Criminal Justice
Recent Scholarship

Edited by
Marilyn McShane and Frank P. Williams III

A Series from LFB Scholarly

Working Mothers and Juvenile Delinquency

Thomas Vander Ven

LFB Scholarly Publishing LLC
New York 2003

#5227/600

Library of Congress Cataloging-in-Publication Data

Vander Ven, Thomas, 1966-
  Working mothers and juvenile delinquency / Thomas Vander Ven.
      p. cm. -- (Criminal justice, recent scholarship)
  Includes bibliographical references and index.
   ISBN 1-931202-72-9 (alk. paper)
   1. Working mothers--United States. 2. Juvenile delinquency--United
States. I. Title. II. Criminal justice (LFB Scholarly Publishing LLC)
  HQ759.48.V36 2003
   306.874'3--dc21

2003011171

ISBN 1-931202-72-9

Printed on acid-free 250-year-life paper.

Manufactured in the United States of America.

TABLE OF CONTENTS

ACKNOWLEDGEMENTS

I owe a tremendous debt of gratitude to my two mentors, Francis T. Cullen and Mark Colvin. This project would not have been possible without their supportive guidance, their high expectations of me, and their unconditional friendship. They are world-class criminology scholars and even better men. Special thanks go to my friends and colleagues in the Department of Sociology and Anthropology at Ohio University. Finally, I want to thank my extended family for their support over the years. And, as always, this work is dedicated to Marikay, Tory, and Sam.

CHAPTER ONE

Social Change, Maternal Employment, and Child Behavior

Research on the causes and consequences of recent changes in the American family has produced a wealth of important, if often conflicting, empirical research findings. After several decades of studying major transformations in family life, researchers still routinely clash over whether the family is truly in decline, with increasingly negative consequences for children, or whether family forms are in many ways changing for the better, in which case public policy should be pointed at supporting the "new family".

Family scholars do seem to agree on the principle forces underlying the metamorphosis of the family: wide scale economic shifts and changes in the composition of the paid workforce since World War II have had a dramatic impact on the forms, stability, and everyday functioning of family life. One of the most dramatic changes is the unprecedented number of women who have entered the paid workforce since the 1970s, which has had a profound impact on the ways in which families operate. Female labor force participation has increased dramatically in recent decades. According to census data, the proportion of women working outside the home has grown from approximately 28 percent in 1940 to close to 60 percent in 1992 (U.S. Bureau of Census 1993). Recent estimates show that well over half of those mothers with children less than one year old are employed outside the home and over 60 percent of those with children younger than three are employed (Bureau of Labor Statistics 2000).

1

Today, widespread maternal employment stimulates much public debate in magazine and newspaper editorials (Dionne 2002; Kristol 1996; Strubel 1996), talk radio, and prime-time news specials. Recently, the potential negative effects of maternal employment were debated in a Long Island newspaper following the tragic shootings at a Colorado high school, with a letter to the editor suggesting that the Littleton massacre was directly related to the absence and neglect of working mothers (see Suffolk Life 1999).

Public concerns about the consequences of working mothers are also reflected in the expansive body of research pointed at the relationship between the employment status of mothers and various outcomes for children. While a large body of research has focused on the potential effects of maternal employment on children's development, few researchers have investigated the possible link between working mothers and delinquent involvement in their children. This neglect is surprising because it became politically fashionable in the 1980s and 1990s to attribute many social problems, including the high rate of U.S. crime, to the general decline of the family.

Despite claims that working mothers are more likely to produce delinquent children, there is little evidence of such a direct effect. In fact, past research findings on the relationship between maternal employment and delinquency have, thus far, been equivocal. At this point, it is unclear whether or not maternal employment is related to delinquency, and we know little about the process through which mother's work and delinquency might be connected.

A deeper understanding of the manner in which mother's work is related to delinquency is needed for several reasons. First, survey researchers have discovered a fairly widespread belief that children are more likely to have behavioral problems, including delinquency, if their mothers work. Greenberger, Goldberg, Crawford and Granger, for example, found in one sample that over 40 percent of their respondents agreed with the statement that teenagers get into less trouble with the law if their mothers do not work full time outside the home" (1988:46). In light of this popular belief, there is a need for empirical research to produce evidence that may challenge or illuminate the validity of an important public concern. At present, there are few research studies that have critically examined the assumed relationship between maternal employment and delinquency. Taken together, the findings produced by those who have studied this issue provide an inconclusive picture of the effects of maternal employment on delinquent involvement. While some investigators have detected a small, positive relationship between maternal employment and delinquency (Glueck and Glueck 1950; Haurin 1992; Hirschi 1969), other researchers have found no relationship (Broidy 1995; Hillman and Sawilowsky 1991; Riege 1972; Roy 1963). Some scholars have even found the children of working mothers to be less delinquent than other children (e.g., Farnworth 1984; West 1982).

The maternal employment-delinquency issue is far from settled. The importance of generating solid evidence regarding the link between mother's work and delinquency continues to grow in our present political climate. Maternal employment will only increase in the coming decade because new welfare legislation will push 50 percent of the present welfare caseload into paid employment (Edin and Lein 1997). Current welfare rolls have dropped to nearly half of their levels in the 1990s and many relatively unskilled, undereducated mothers are being moved into the paid labor market (Sherman et al.1998). Understanding the link between maternal employment and child outcomes is especially critical for this population because most mothers making the transition from welfare to work will be taking low-status, low-paying jobs, which may have negative effects on mothers and their families. On the other hand, the welfare to work transition may well benefit mothers and children in many ways. In order to appreciate the differential effects of different kinds of paid employment and welfare-reliance on child outcomes, more research is needed in this area.

A second reason to explore the relationship between maternal employment and delinquency is that existing studies have produced findings which are often difficult to interpret due to the use of limited data sets, due to narrow operationalizations of mother's work, and due to a failure to specify the process through which maternal employment might be criminogenic. As I will argue more fully in the pages ahead, detecting the effects of maternal employment on delinquency will be best accomplished by considering a wide variety of maternal work characteristics (e.g., hours employed, working conditions, pay), by investigating many different avenues through which mother's work affects delinquency, and by using longitudinal data to examine the relationship between the timing of maternal work and delinquency. Past researchers have largely ignored these issues.

Third, in addition to addressing the dearth of comprehensive research on this issue, a better understanding of the relationship between mother's work and delinquent behavior will help to add insight into the effects of larger social structural factors on family life and delinquency. Linking social structure to the family is important because an emerging body of research findings has shown that criminal behavior can usually be traced to early childhood experiences (see Benson 2002). Because the family acts as the principle agent of socialization for children, research on the origins of antisocial and criminal behavior has often focused on parenting. As a result of scores of research studies on the linkages between parenting styles and behaviors and delinquency, we now know that, among other factors, lax supervision, parental neglect, and ineffective discipline are consistent predictors of delinquency (Benson 2002; Loeber and Stouthamer-Loeber 1986; also Wright and Wright 1995). The relationship between family processes and delinquency is well established; however, conspicuously missing from theory and research on family and delinquency are the antecedent structural factors that shape family life.

A focus on the effect of mother's work on delinquency is an important step toward understanding the structural forces that influence family processes and delinquency because one of the most immediately impinging structural force on the life of a parent is his or her job. In the U.S., as in other industrial nations, work is the "central identifier of the self" (Gamst 1995). Employment embeds people in society, providing opportunity for stable social interaction and giving them a resource for identifying themselves to others and for evaluating self-worth. But work is much more than a resource for identity. Jobs are powerful social forces because they provide the wages on which families subsist, because they directly affect the self-concept and mental health of parents, and because "work constitutes a framework for daily behavior and patterns of interaction because it imposes disciplines and regularities" upon parents, which shape the manner in which they raise their children (Wilson 1996:73).

Family researchers have long recognized the fluid boundaries between work and family life, but criminologists have largely ignored the potential relationship between parental work, family process, and the behavior of children (for notable exceptions see Colvin 2000; Colvin and Pauly 1983; Messner and Krohn 1990; Simpson and Elis 1990). The neglect of the work-family link is part of a larger theoretical problem within criminology. That is, theorists and researchers tend to focus on the criminogenic effects of faulty family processes without recognizing the broader social conditions that affect the family. Currie has referred to this manner of thinking as the "fallacy of autonomy"--the belief that what goes on inside the family can be meaningfully separated from the forces that affect it from the outside (1985:185). An extensive body of research reveals that families present children with a variety of powerful risk factors that influence delinquent involvement. To improve our understanding of the relationship between family and delinquency, however, we must also investigate the structural factors that influence the health and organization of the family. Specifically, greater attention is needed to the ways in which patterns and conditions of employment contribute to crime. As Currie has argued, in order to bring clarity to our knowledge about the causes of crime and how to reduce it, "it is time to start thinking about work" (1993:51).

Given these considerations, this study attempts to assess the importance of work as it relates to delinquency by exploring the impact of maternal employment status and maternal working conditions on youths' behavior. The present study attempts to advance past research on mother's work and delinquency in several ways. First, past researchers have usually treated maternal employment as a dichotomous status; that is, most of the studies investigating mother's work and delinquency have simply compared the delinquency of children who have "working" mothers to the delinquency of children who have "non-working" mothers. This method of analysis fails to capture the wide variability of hours worked by mothers who are employed. This research attempts to present a more systematic analysis by including mothers who work part-time, mothers who work full-time, and mothers who work over-time hours. It is important to consider variations in time spent in employment outside the home because the number of hours worked may influence the quantity and quality of time that mothers spend with their children. Hours worked could also have an impact on the emotional and psychological conditions of mothers with consequences for child rearing.

Second, past investigators have treated "working" mothers as if they were all employed in the same occupation with identical wages, working conditions, benefits, and employment policies. By simply dividing mothers into two categories--those who work and those who do not--researchers seem to be arguing that maternal employment only matters to the extent that work draws mothers away from parenting duties. There is little recognition that working conditions vary greatly and that different types of jobs may affect family processes and delinquency differently. Following the pioneering work of Kohn (1977), researchers have found that employment conditions have consequences for the attitudes, mental health, and parenting styles of workers. It may be, then, that maternal employment is most strongly related to delinquency when mothers have stressful jobs, perform duties that are lacking in complexity or autonomy, or have inflexible work schedules. Coercive, unsatisfying, and inflexible jobs may negatively shape parent-child relations and thus contribute to behavior problems in children.

Third, just as scholars interested in maternal employment and delinquency have regarded "working" mothers as a homogenous group, so have they represented non-working mothers as a uniform set. The implicit assumption made in previous studies is that non-working mothers are similar in that their primary time investment is in child-rearing and domestic duties. This assumption that non-working mothers are homogenous fails to consider the various forms of financial resources that these mothers potentially draw upon. While some non-working mothers draw financial support from a cohabitating spouse or partner, others rely on funding from other family sources or rely on welfare. These differences are important because whether a non-working mother draws financial support from family sources or from welfare should have consequences for her self-concept, for her mental health, and for the home environment in which children are raised (Parcel 1996). The differences between various types of non-working mothers and between various types of working mothers will be studied by including welfare-reliant mothers, non-working mothers who are not on welfare, and working mothers in the analysis. Previous research on maternal employment and delinquency has not investigated the wide range of working and non-working mothers that will be included in the present study.

The final way in which this study seeks to improve upon past explorations into the maternal employment-delinquency relationship is by drawing from a variety of theoretical perspectives to guide the analysis. Thus far, little theoretical development has taken place regarding the relationship between mother's work and delinquency. In the past, researchers have tended to view this relationship predominantly through the lens of social control theory. Embracing the social control perspective, the dominant assumption has been that working mothers may be inhibited from supervising or monitoring their children directly (Broidy 1995; Haurin 1992; Hirschi 1969; Nye 1963; Roy 1963; Sampson and Laub 1993) or from forging strong parent-child bonds that function as informal social controls against delinquency (Hirschi 1969; Riege 1972). Parental control may be one important pathway through which mother's work influences delinquent involvement; however, the overemphasis on social control theory has limited researchers in their ability to explain the relationship. The contentions of research informed by the social control orientation broaden the theoretical scope of this analysis by introducing insights from three perspectives: social support theory (Cullen 1994); social stress theory (e.g., McLoyd 1989; Menaghan, Kowaleski-Jones, and Mott 1997); and class-related explanations for the relationship between work, family, and behavioral problems (e.g., Colvin and Pauly 1983; Rogers, Parcel, and Menaghan 1991).

Social support theory (Cullen 1994) contributes to the present analysis because it includes the argument that parents influence the behavior of children not only through control mechanisms, but also by providing the expressive and instrumental supports for children that lower the risks of delinquent involvement. Maternal employment, then, may affect delinquency by reducing the quantity of time that mothers spend nurturing and giving affection to children, or by inhibiting mothers from assisting children with personal problems or investing time in children's school work. Social support theory adds potential explanatory power to the current analysis and provides a competing or complementary explanation to the social control perspective. Accordingly, it is possible that mother's employment works through parental support to influence delinquency.

The social stress perspective informs the current study through its assertion that parents who are psychologically distressed by work experiences often find that family relations are negatively affected as a result (Menaghan, Kowaleski-Jones, and Mott 1997). This insight helps to bridge the gap between job conditions and family life by recognizing that work-related stress is often carried into the home, which in turn could strain family relations and negatively influence child outcomes.

A final explanatory scheme for the effects of maternal employment on delinquency will be constructed based upon Colvin and Pauly's structural-Marxist theory of delinquency production (1983; see also Colvin 2000). Colvin and Pauly argue that parents who are controlled through coercive mechanisms in the workplace are likely to control their children in a similarly coercive fashion. Coercively controlled children, then, form alienated bonds to parents, which have consequences for later behaviors in school, makes children more likely to form delinquent peer associations, and raises the probability of delinquent involvement (1983). The process described by Colvin and Pauly (1983) will be investigated by tracing the effects of maternal working conditions on delinquency through maternal disciplinary style, parent-child attachment, and delinquent peer associations. Past empirical tests of this theory have used cross-sectional data and have found only weak to moderate support for the theoretical predictions (Messner and Krohn 1990; Simpson and Elis 1990). While this study will not involve a direct test of the theory, it will improve upon past efforts by employing the use of longitudinal data to capture the predicted temporal process linking parent's work, family processes, and juvenile delinquency.

The aforementioned theoretical insights guided my analysis of the potential avenues through which maternal employment may influence delinquency by shaping and constraining parenting behaviors and affecting the general quality of familial relations. The longitudinal nature of the data also allows assessment of the extent to which these processes are influenced by the timing of maternal employment. The importance of timing in maternal employment is examined for possible effects of mother's current work and any effects of early maternal work (i.e., employment occurring in the child's pre-school years) on family life and delinquency. By including a wide range of working and non-working mothers and by considering maternal working conditions and the timing of mother's employment, this study attempts to present a comprehensive examination of the relationship between maternal employment and delinquency.

Social Change, Women, and Work

One of the more common concerns about family transformation is that women have been increasingly drawn into the workforce and away from their childrearing responsibilities. Surveys have found that many Americans believe that children are negatively affected when their mothers are employed outside the home. Greenberger et al. (1988), for example, found that 40% of respondents believed that children formed less secure attachments with their working mothers, 47 percent believed that children perform better in school if their mothers do not work, and 57 percent believed that children of working mothers suffer emotionally because mothers are not there when they need them. Undoubtedly, family life has been changed dramatically due to the massive increase of women entering the labor force in the 1970s and 1980s. Census data show that female labor force participation rose from approximately 28 percent in 1940 (Blau and Ferber 1986) to close to 60% in 1992 (U.S. Bureau of Census 1993). With this wave of women entering the labor force came an unprecedented number of working mothers. Maternal employment has increased from 40 percent in 1970 to over 70 percent today. Currently, over half of the those with children less than one year old are employed outside the home (Collins and Coltrane 1995; Gerson 1996) and over 60 percent of those with children younger than six are employed (Gormley 1995).

There are a number of explanations for the large increase in female labor participation. First, women began to enter the work force at record rates because of the financial strains families faced in the early 1970s. The decline in well-paying manufacturing jobs, along with an increase in poorly compensated service sector jobs and rising unemployment rates, resulted in a decline in real family income from 1973 to 1988 (Gormley 1995; Scarr,

Phillips, and McCartney 1994). During this period, female employment became necessary for many families to avoid poverty.

Second, the increase in divorce and a rise in never-married mothers over the last three decades forced more women to seek employment to care for their families (Gormley 1995). Because divorced, separated, and widowed women are more likely to work than married women (U.S. Census Bureau 1993), a rise in marital dissolution should be accompanied by an increase in female labor participation. This relationship also works in the opposite direction, with a rise in female labor participation resulting in an increase in divorce.

Third, the women's liberation movement created greater access to education and employment and inspired women to seek self-actualization through obtaining advanced degrees and making full-time careers (Scarr, Phillips and McCartney 1994). The intersection of changing cultural beliefs about gender roles and a growth of opportunities for female careers outside of the home helped to produce the unprecedented wave of women who entered the labor market in the 1960s and 1970s (Gormley 1995).

These trends are likely to persist throughout the new century. As real wages remain stagnant, marital dissolution stays high, and female-headed families continue to become more common, more mothers are expected to take full-time employment. It is probably no longer relevant to ask whether or not women "should" work. Although most working mothers report that they want to be employed (Scarr, Phillips and McCartney 1994), census data suggest that only one out of ten American women feel that staying out of the labor force is even a financially feasible option (Reeves 1992) and recent surveys show that over 75 percent of working women report that their income is essential to the support of their family (Hall 1995). This need for paid employment is especially true of single mothers who must work to avoid poverty.

The Quality and General Conditions of "Women's Work": Why Should Mother's Employment Affect Child Outcomes?

Although women have gained greater access to jobs in the labor market over the last two decades, gender inequality in the workplace still predominates. The average wage, working conditions, and general social valuation of jobs primarily held by women compare unfavorably with the characteristics of male-dominated occupations (see Dubeck and Borman 1996; Reskin and Padavic 1994). Parcel and Menaghan (1994) have argued that the characteristics of a mother's job may have a more powerful effect than the conditions of a father's job given greater maternal involvement with young children, even among dual-earner families. When two parents are present, both mother and father contribute to the overall development of their offspring. In fact, fathers have been found to be increasingly critical to healthy development as children enter adolescence (Furstenberg 1994; Lamb 1981; Rossi 1985). However, because women do tend to interact with infants and younger children at a greater rate, and due to the growth in mother-only families over the last two decades, it is critical to examine fully the impact of mother's employment on the lives of children.

According to Reskin and Padavic (1994), gender inequality in the labor market can be broken down into four categories: sex segregation, the "pay gap," the "promotions gap," and the "authority gap." Sex segregation refers to the fact that certain jobs and occupations are sex-typed in that they are largely filled by male or female incumbents. For example, "Secretary" was the most common occupation for women in 1990, but it did not make the top ten for male workers (Reskin and Padavic 1994). Furthermore, female workers tend to be clustered in occupations that offer low wages (e.g., secretary, office clerk, retail sales). The "pay gap," which refers to the fact that among full-time paid workers, women earn no more than 70 percent of what men earn (Parcel and Menaghan 1994), is one of the consequences of sex segregation (Reskin and Padavic 1994). Research consistently shows that women pay an earnings penalty by simply being employed in female-dominated occupations (England, Herbert, Kilbourne, Reid, and Megdal 1994; Jacobs and Steinberg 1990).

The "promotions gap" refers to the fact that women appear to be at a decided disadvantage with respect to career advancement when compared to men. This phenomenon, known as the "glass ceiling" effect, exists across industries and occupations. Researchers have found that women are much less likely than men to be promoted in Fortune 500 companies (Fierman 1990), private industry in general (Reskin and Padavic 1994), and in the public sector as well (Cohen 1996). This promotion gap can be explained, in part, by women being segregated in industries and occupations characterized by low-mobility, and by women having lower levels of human capital (Reskin and Padavic 1994). Researchers have found, however, that some portion of the career advantages of men cannot be explained by these variables, which suggests that discrimination contributes to the promotion disparity (e.g., Bellas 1994; Rosenfeld 1980).

Similarly, women are much less likely than men to be in positions of authority. Occupational authority refers to having the organizationally granted power to make important decisions, control resources, and to supervise and lead other workers. Lacking the power to make decisions about the content of their jobs, women tend to have more repetitive jobs with less opportunity to exercise initiative or to apply high-level skills to their work (Hodson and

Sullivan 1990). This inequality, too, can be explained by the sex segregation of the workplace, human capital differences, and discrimination (Reskin and Padavic 1994).

Because women are more likely to have less complex, lower-paying jobs, with less chance for advancement and less opportunity to exercise authority or initiative, it might lead to the prediction that women have lower levels of job satisfaction. Research shows, however, that women are at least as satisfied, if not more satisfied, than their male counterparts (Hodson 1989; Mortimer and Lawrence 1995). Although the processes affecting job satisfaction are similar for both men and women, female job satisfaction appears to be more closely dependent on family variables. Coverman (1989) found, for example, that women are more likely to be dissatisfied with their job when they experience conflict between family and work roles or competing demands from children and husbands. Similarly, job dissatisfaction may enhance work-family conflict directly by negatively influencing the affective states of working mothers. Stressful and unsatisfying work can reduce marital quality and contribute to family conflict (Pearlin and McCall 1990) and can produce maternal stress that may result in strained parent-child relations (MacEwen and Barling 1991). Conversely, research suggests that those mothers who are satisfied with their jobs and experience less work-family conflict are less likely to have strained relations with their children and less likely to have children with behavioral problems (e.g., Paulson 1996)

The general devaluation and inequality faced by working women has consequences extending beyond job satisfaction. If working mothers often occupy positions of low complexity, low autonomy, and low control over workplace activities, research suggests that they should also experience damage to psychological functioning, physical health, and general well-being (Lennon 1994; Link, Lennon, and Dohrenwend 1993; Kohn and Schooler 1982;

Turner, Wheaton, and Lloyd 1995). Work-related psychological distress may be a critical factor in shaping the degree to which mothers nurture, support, and effectively discipline their children (Pett, Vaughan-Cole, and Wampold 1994).

These insights have influenced a generation of researchers. Kohn's (1977) theory and research on the work-family link were critical to the formulation of Colvin and Pauly's (1983) structural-Marxist theory of delinquency production. Colvin and Pauly (1983) theorized that serious patterned delinquency is most common among lower-class youths because of the coercive workplace controls that their parents experience in their jobs which in turn affect the way children are socialized in the home. Drawing from Edwards's (1979) work on occupational control structures and Kohn's (1977) research on the effects of working conditions on parenting, they theorize that parents in the lowest class fraction experience coercive job controls, which drive them to treat their children in a similarly coercive manner. Children raised under authoritarian and often erratic conditions, then, develop alienated bonds toward authority, misbehave in school settings, and are subsequently grouped with other conduct-disordered children where they form delinquent peer groups. Although empirical tests of this model have generated mixed results (Messner and Krohn 1990; Simpson and Elis 1990), this theory could lend important concepts to understanding the link between mother's working conditions and delinquency in their children. The workplace control dimension is particularly relevant for investigating the link between maternal employment and delinquency because women, especially Black females, are heavily overrepresented in low-wage, coercively controlled occupations in the lowest class fraction (Edwards 1979; Menaghan 1991).

The idea that workplace controls are related to behavioral problems in children of working mothers is supported by empirical research. Rogers, Parcel, and Menaghan (1991) found that mothers who worked under conditions of simple control--the method used in the lowest class fraction-- were more likely than others to report disruptive, disobedient, and antisocial behavior in their children. Similarly, Parcel and Menaghan (1991, 1994) found that the occupational complexity of mother's work positively influenced the home environment and that working mothers with simple, repetitive jobs (low in occupational complexity) were less able than other mothers to prevent behavioral problems in their children. These effects remained even when controlling for maternal age, maternal education, and maternal AFQT score (Parcel and Menaghan 1991).

General working conditions may affect the mother-child relationship in other ways. Occupational conditions are likely to have an effect on the level of intrapersonal stress experienced by working mothers, which in turn should influence the quality of relations with children and parental perceptions of behavioral problems in children. For example, parents with low-status jobs in the service-sector are more vulnerable to job loss and less insulated from economic setbacks due to the lack of union organization and due to less protective legislation in these jobs (McLoyd 1990).

In many ways, the working conditions of mothers may influence the quality of parent-child interaction. An equally important issue is the relationship between maternal employment and the quantity of time that mothers spend with children. When mothers work, children may suffer due to inadequate or ineffective non-parental care or because the absence of mothers weakens the mother-child bond. Because bonds between parents and children serve as important inhibitors of delinquent behavior, it is important to consider the possibility that the children of working mothers are less attached to mothers and thus are, thus more free to act in deviant ways. Existing literature on the effects of non-parental care outlines some of the ways in which extra-familial care may contribute to delinquent behavior.

Non-Parental Child Care

The present study will focus upon the effects of maternal employment that takes place early in a child's life and on the effects of maternal employment that takes place when children are adolescents. The timing of employment is relevant in part because it relates to the form (i.e., the providers) that social control and social support takes in the absence of parents. Research in the growing field of developmental criminology shows that investigators must build theoretical models that include age-specific risk factors tailored to capture the unique problems children face at different maturational stages (see Benson 2002).

With respect to maternal employment, it should be recognized that pre-school children may form insecure attachments when mothers are occupied outside of the home, while teenage children may experience more freedom to participate in unsupervised activities with peer groups, to establish and maintain delinquent peer associations, and to organize their activities beyond the purview of adult monitoring. Adolescents may also suffer a different kind of maternal deprivation. In addition to a reduction in direct control, the teen children of working mothers may suffer a reduction in parental support. Job obligations may inhibit mothers from discussing problems with adolescents, helping them with schoolwork, or attending their extra-curricular activities such as athletic events or music performances. If work obligations prevent mothers from being cognizant of their child's after-school activities and peer associations, and reduce the mother's capacity as a resource for support, then we should expect maternal work to be positively associated to delinquency.

Pre-school children of working mothers may face a variety of risk factors during their first years of life. If developing a secure, trusting attachment to one's mother is indeed the first critical milestone in human development (Erikson 1959), and then any threat to that bond posed by maternal deprivation must be considered an early risk factor. Because some researchers have found weak mother-child attachments and antisocial behavior in children cared for in supplemental care settings during the first years of life (see Belsky and Rovine 1988; see Hoffman 1989), there is reason to examine this possible relationship.

Others have suggested that the amount of time spent in extra-familial care is less important than the quality of that care (Clarke-Stewart 1989). Because the data set used for the present study lacks good information on the form or quality of non-parental care, this study will focus on the extent to which the quantity of time spent away from mothers early in life influences parent-child bonds, parent-child relations, and later delinquency. Although the quality of non-parental child care cannot be examined in this study, I will briefly discuss past research in this area in order to highlight the range of concerns related to maternal employment and outcomes for children.

In this work, child care is defined as "a regularly used arrangement for supervising young children that supplements care by one or both parents" (Gormley 1995). For pre-school and prepubescent school-age children, non-parental child care most commonly comes in the form of a relative, neighbor, babysitter, or an organized child care center. For adolescents, child care should be seen in a much broader sense; that is, teenagers acquire an increasingly longer leash as they mature and develop, but are still in need of and subject to various forms of social control. While most teenagers are unlikely to report to a babysitter or daycare facility every day after school, they do experience varying levels of control and support as provided by parents, close relatives, neighbors, teachers, coaches, police and other adult members of the community.

Concern for the children of working mothers may be traced to the World War II era when social commentators feared that the scores of women who went to work for the defense industry were leaving their children unattended, unsupervised, and unsafe (Louv 1990). The need for alternative modes of child care did not go away when the war ended. Rosie the Riveter's daughters were even more likely to join the labor force and to spend longer hours away from their young children.

In 1970, the White House Conference on Children proclaimed child care the most serious problem faced by American families (Zigler 1989). Today, the need for more and better child care is often referred to as a national crisis (Reeves 1992; Zigler 1989). Among the problems which constitute this crisis are: many U.S. children are currently being cared for in unhealthy, unsafe, and unstimulating environments; many families are unable to secure appropriate child care because of work schedules or because of having chronically-ill, disabled, or school-aged children; and the fact that economically disadvantaged families are blocked from procuring quality care for their children because of financial limitations (Reeves 1992).

As female labor participation has grown, so too has research on the effects of supplemental child care on children (Parcel and Menaghan 1994). Much of the earliest, and most controversial, work in this area was produced by Jay Belsky and his colleagues (see Belsky and Rovine 1988). Known as the "infant day care controversy" (Fox and Fein 1990), child care researchers argued over Belsky's early findings that extra-parental child care during the first years of life was detrimental to the development of children.

Belsky has argued that child care studies show a negative effect of early supplement care on certain developmental outcomes. Specifically, he notes that children who spent more than 20 hours per week in supplemental care during their first year of life were less likely to form secure attachments to their mothers (Belsky and Rovine 1988; Jacobson and Wille 1984; Vaughn, Gore, and Egeland 1980) and were more likely to display antisocial behavior during peer interaction and non-compliant behavior with adults (Belsky and Eggebeen 1991; Haskins 1985; Schwarz, Strickland, and Krolick 1974).

These findings stimulated a flood of critical responses, often focused on the perceived methodological inadequacies of Belsky's work (see Scarr and Eisenberg 1993 for review of findings; See also Harvey 1999). Other researchers (e.g., Clarke-Stewart 1988) produced findings that contradict Belsky's assertions about the negative effects of nonparental care. In fact, recently, a research team announced that preliminary findings from a longitudinal study on the effects of supplemental child care found that infants in nonparental daycare are as securely attached to mothers as infants cared for by mothers in the home (Chira 1996).

Any relationship between supplemental child care and child outcomes is a complex one that requires a focus on a wide variety of contextual factors. According to Parcel and Menaghan (1994), child care research is no longer simplistically concerned with the differences in outcomes between children raised in the home by full-time mothers and children receiving supplemental care. Researchers have moved beyond group comparisons to examine the effects of qualitative differences in child care arrangements on children. Volumes of work have been published on the need for "higher quality" child care. Although there is no clear consensus on the precise characteristics of a "quality" child care arrangement (Moss and Pence 1994), researchers tend to focus on a few salient dimensions: caregiver-child ratios, quality of interaction between caregivers and children, stability of care, appropriate curriculum and staff training, and attention to health and safety requirements (Scarr and Eisenberg 1993).

Child care is seen as less effective as the ratio of children to caregivers increases. The caregiver-child ratio, then, is often examined in order to assess the quality of formal child care. Research shows that high child-to-caregiver ratios can be damaging to development because caregivers spend less time directly involved with any given child (Parcel and Menaghan 1994). Reduced one-on-one attention can hurt a child by limiting opportunities to learn and to expand his or her cognitive capacity. Furthermore, when ratios are high, children have more opportunity to form counter-normative peer groups within the formal care setting (Parcel and Menaghan 1994). The development of an attachment to formal rules and pro-social norms, then, is increasingly threatened as the numbers of children outpace the numbers of responsible adults.

In a review of research on child care, Scarr and Eisenberg (1993) reported that children in child care benefit when class sizes are smaller, when caregiver-child ratios are lower, when caregivers are trained in child development, and when turnover, a sign of instability, is low. Additionally, research shows that extra-familial child care can promote normal, healthy development in children, but that the influence of child care experiences cannot be examined outside of the characteristics of a child's family and home (Scarr and Eisenberg 1993). Gamble and Zigler (1986), for example, found that supplemental child care interacts with family environmental factors, such as family conflict and father absence, to influence outcomes in children. In short, low-quality child care in early childhood tends to negatively affect those children who are experiencing risk factors in the home. Poor quality care should be seen as an element of an additive model of childhood risks (Scarr and Eisenberg 1993).

It is difficult, therefore to separate the effects of a child's home environment from the effects of a child care setting. Research has found that more punitive, authoritarian parents tend to select lower quality child care for their children (Scarr and Eisenberg 1993) and that children who come from structurally disadvantaged homes (i.e., single, low-income mothers) or functionally disorganized homes are more likely to be placed by parents in low quality child care settings (Howes and Olenick 1986).

This fact makes studying the effects of child care problematic. As Parcel and Menaghan (1994) point out, "nonmaternal care arrangements are apt to reflect other existing inequalities among families. For this reason as well it may be difficult to isolate a significant independent effect of child care variables..." (1994: 191). Inequality may well be reproduced when financially limited parents are forced to place their children in lower quality care settings, which could promote developmental deficits and subsequent behavioral problems (Brayfield et al. 1993; Larner and Phillips 1994). The quality of child care could have consequences for later delinquent involvement through its effect on the cognitive, emotional, and social development of children. High quality child care should promote academic proficiency, social abilities, and conflict resolution skills, all of which might insulate children from delinquent pressures.

Maternal Employment and Delinquency

Social scientists have warned of the potential relationship between maternal employment and problematic behavior in children. Coleman (1988), for example, argued that children of working mothers may suffer from the absence of social capital. To Coleman, social capital is a parent's investment in his or her child that involves time, physical proximity, and energy, and that is critical for the transmission of norms and prosocial behavior to children (Parcel and Menaghan 1994).

The study of maternal employment and delinquency has focused similarly on the importance of a mother's involvement with children and on the consequences of a working mother's reduced physical presence. It has often been assumed that working mothers are "not around" to nurture and supervise their developing children, which could result in behavioral problems or delinquency. While past research has produced mixed results that are sometimes difficult to interpret, investigators have revealed some provocative issues that deserve further exploration.

The first issue developed by previous research relates to the causal process linking mother's work to delinquency. Although most researchers have assumed that maternal employment may be criminogenic because it reduces maternal supervision of adolescents, research findings have cast some doubt on this assumption. I will discuss the research studies that emphasize supervision and those studies that have looked beyond supervision to predict the effects of mother's work. These studies provide insights that will be used to inform the analysis in this study.

The second issue raised by previous research relates to a potential class-dependent effect of maternal employment on behavioral problems in children. Researchers have produced findings that imply that mother's work may have different effects depending on the socioeconomic class of the family.   The possibility that the effects of maternal employment are class-dependent will be explored in this study by examining the causal processes linking different classes of workers to different outcomes for children.

A third issue developed by past research points to the importance of family structure as a possible influence on the maternal employment-delinquency relationship. Investigators have found that maternal employment may have different associations to child behavior depending upon whether working mothers are single (i.e., unmarried, divorced, widowed, separated) or married and co-residing with a spouse. This issue will be explored in the current study by examining the effects of maternal employment within single-mother and married-mother sub-groups.

Social Control Explanations for the Effects of Maternal Employment

Social control explanations for the relationship between maternal work and delinquency have dominated past research in this area. In fact, maternal employment has sometimes been used as a proxy for direct parental supervision. In such research, investigators assume that having an employed mother reduces the extent to which a child is directly monitored. Broidy (1995), for instance, included a variable that reflected the extent to which mothers worked when study children were growing up to compare an indirect measure of direct supervision with more direct measures of supervision such as parental monitoring. Broidy (1995) found no relationship between maternal employment and delinquency in her sample. Because the author was only interested in maternal employment as an alternative measure of direct supervision, Broidy's (1995) operationalization of maternal employment was limited. Study children were asked to report how much their mothers worked when they were growing up--not at all, some of the time, nearly all of the time. No consideration is given to the type of work that mothers do, the impact that work has upon mother's affective states, or to some of the family processes beyond direct supervision that might be influenced by mother's work.

Riege (1972) followed a similar line of inquiry, using maternal employment status as a measure of maternal separation. The author theorized that young girls with working mothers might suffer maternal deprivation as a result. Lacking maternal guidance and supervision, the daughters of employed mothers were thought to be more prone to delinquent involvement. Riege (1972) failed to find differences related to maternal employment when comparing twenty-five girls living in a correctional facility to twenty-five non-delinquent girls. These findings contribute relatively little to knowledge about the effects of maternal employment because the nature of and size of her sample make it difficult to extend her conclusions to a larger population and because her limited measure of maternal employment fails to capture any variability in maternal employment.

As with the studies by Broidy (1995) and Riege (1972), the earliest research on maternal employment and delinquency was informed by a social control orientation. Investigators assumed that working mothers might produce wayward children because they were not supervising them closely enough. Glueck and Glueck (1950), for example, found that more of the mothers of delinquents than of non-delinquents worked outside the home and claimed that this relationship "means that more of the children in the families of delinquents were deprived of maternal supervision" (1950:112).

Consistent with this argument was the Gluecks' finding that the relationship between maternal employment and delinquency disappeared when controlling for the level of supervision that working mothers were able to arrange through alternative child-care sources for their children. A close examination of the Gluecks' data, however, suggests that supervision may not be the only intervening link between maternal employment and delinquency. Among the children of employed mothers, the most delinquent group was those who had occasionally employed mothers as opposed to regularly employed mothers. If maternal supervision was the sole link between mother's work and delinquency, then work commitment (the amount of time spent in outside employment) should be related to delinquency in a linear fashion---the mothers who work the most should supervise children the least resulting in the highest probability of delinquency.

The Gluecks (1950) attempted to explain the highest rate of delinquency in the occasionally employed group by arguing that occasionally employed mothers might be those who work out of boredom and caprice as a way to avoid household drudgery; such mothers do not work out of necessity but out of indifference to their maternal duties. According to the authors, occasionally employed mothers, then, are neglectful mothers. This thesis is never examined further but implies that maternal employment may work through causal mechanisms beyond direct control.

Contrary to the Gluecks' (1950) findings, Hirschi (1969) found a linear relationship between mother's employment and delinquency. Delinquency was least likely among the children of housewives, more likely among children of part-time employed mothers, and most common among the children of full-time employed mothers. Hirschi (1969) hypothesized that this relationship owed to some aspect of direct supervision but found that the relationship remained intact after controlling for supervision and for mother-child attachment. In light of this development, Hirschi (1969) suggested that maternal employment is linked to delinquency in some more subtle way. He argued that an employed mother may be a less compelling source of conscience than a non-employed mother whose presence in the home is a more persistent reminder of a child's duty to good behavior. In other words, even when an adolescent is away from home, a non-employed mother may "seem" closer in proximity and more able to detect misbehavior than a mother who is busy at work might be. Hirschi's suggestion that maternal employment may weaken indirect controls, such as a child's conscience, was not investigated in his sample, but suggests that researchers should look beyond supervision to explain the association between maternal employment and delinquency.

In contrast to the dominant theoretical emphasis on direct controls, Sampson and Laub (1993; 1994) traced the effects of maternal employment on delinquency through a variety of family process variables and through child's school attachment, school performance, and delinquent peer association. The authors found that maternal employment was not significantly associated with delinquency when other factors were controlled, but was significantly linked to a decrease in supervision. The authors maintained that mother's employment outside the home has no discernible, direct effect on delinquency, but can be criminogenic if employment keeps mothers from properly supervising their children. Furthermore, the authors detected a negative effect of mother's employment on school attachment. This is an important finding because it points to another possible avenue through which mother's work influences delinquency. Several studies have found that as school attachment increases, the probability of delinquency is reduced (Hirschi 1969; Wiatrowski 1981; Sampson and Laub 1993). This potential path can be explored by tracing the effects of maternal employment on delinquency through school attachment.

Although the Sampson and Laub studies suggest that maternal employment can contribute to delinquent activity by weakening supervision and school attachment, the findings are questionable for a few reasons. First, maternal employment is operationalized as a dichotomous variable. Children of mothers who do not work are compared to mothers with any amount of out-of-home employment. A more realistic range of mother's time spent in outside employment (part-time, full-time, over-time) must be obtained to truly test the relationship.

Second, the Gluecks' sample is appropriate for exploring the association between maternal employment, family processes, and delinquency in the 1940s and 1950s, but their data may not be an acceptable population for studying this phenomenon in the 1990s. As stated previously, women have entered the paid workforce at a record pace since the 1950s and have gained greater access to white-collar occupations, positions of authority, and other jobs with higher pay, autonomy, and better working conditions. To the extent that conditions of work affect parenting styles, we might find that the qualitative advances made in jobs held by women have changed the relationship between women's work and outcomes for children.

Furthermore, the possibilities for finding alternative sources for child care have increased since the Gluecks collected their data. Although finding quality, affordable child care is still seen by many as a national problem (Gormley 1995); the working mother in the 1990s is much more likely to find a consistent source of alternative care and supervision for her child in a structured pre-school or after-school daycare program.

Class, Maternal Employment, and Delinquency

Like the Gluecks (1950), Nye (1963:139) argued that maternal employment and delinquency are related because "employed mothers presumably experience more difficulty in exercising direct control and supervision of children particularly in the 'after school' period." As predicted, Nye (1963) found that the children of employed mothers were more likely to be delinquent than the children of non-employed mothers. The differences between the two groups, however, were small and Nye was unable to explain the effect because he either chose not to or was unable to introduce a statistical control for maternal supervision. He assumed that supervision is the intervening link but did not examine it empirically.

The study by Nye (1963) is particularly significant because it was the first to suggest that the effects of maternal employment may be dependent to some degree on social class. A close look at Nye's (1963) data shows that when the largely middle-class sample is separated into high, medium, and low socioeconomic statuses, the positive effect of maternal employment on delinquency only holds for the middle group. Nye (1963) did not attempt to explain why maternal employment might be criminogenic for middle-class children but not for higher and lower status children. Hoffman (1963), however, has offered an explanation. Hoffman reasoned that the motivations for maternal employment, the nature of the work, and the attitudes of the mother and other family members may be different in the different class statuses. With respect to Hoffman's point about the "nature of work," it may be that maternal employment at the highest status level is most likely professional work that allows for self-direction and schedule flexibility. Better and more flexible working conditions may have a positive effect on the affective states of mothers and could allow them more time to devote to parenting duties.

Hoffman (1963) offered an explanation for why maternal work may be unrelated to delinquency at the highest status levels, but did not address the lack of relationship at the lowest socioeconomic level. To help explain this finding, I now turn to the results of research studies that focused upon maternal work and delinquency in low-income populations.

In a longitudinal study of working-class families, West (1982) found that the sons of working mothers were significantly less likely to be delinquent than the sons of unemployed mothers. He explained this finding by arguing that working mothers effectively increased the family income, which improved the living conditions of their children. Corroboration for this argument can be found in a recent study by Zhao, Cao, and Cao (1997), who found that more maternal work hours were associated with less delinquency in a low-income population.

Similarly, Farnworth (1984) studied the effects of family structure on delinquency in a low-income, minority population and found that youths were less likely to perform certain deviant acts if both parents worked. Specifically, she discovered that children whose mothers were employed when the child was three years old were less likely to engage in forms of escapism (e.g., running away from home and drug use) when they were fifteen. This finding points out that maternal employment should be considered as an economic dimension of family life in addition to being an influence on parenting. As Farnworth (1984) suggests, maternal employment may be most beneficial when the alternative to work is economic disadvantage or welfare dependency. This assumption will be tested in the present study by comparing the effects of maternal employment in the lowest occupational class to the effects of welfare reliance. If the analysis reveals that lower-class, working families experience benefits over welfare-reliant families with respect to family functioning and delinquency, then it will lend support to the notion that maternal employment improves family lives and child outcomes by increasing economic resources of relatively disadvantaged families.

It may be, also, that maternal employment is more conducive to high quality parent-child relations than welfare reliance. Parcel (1996) suggests that welfare reliance, as opposed to paid employment, is associated with lower quality parenting skills. Because these differences might be explained by maternal characteristics which precede welfare or work status (e.g., maternal education, maternal AFQT), proper controls must be introduced to show that parenting differences can be attributed to welfare versus work status. Accordingly, I will include controls for maternal education and maternal AFQT in all analyses.

Like Farnworth (1984) and Zhao, et al., (1997), Haurin (1992) found that maternal employment had a unique effect upon delinquency among relatively disadvantaged sub-groups. Haurin (1992) discovered that having an employed mother increased the odds of marijuana use and serious illegal activity for Blacks and Hispanics but not for Whites. This finding is contrary to the Farnworth (1984) and Zhao et al. (1997) results because it suggests that maternal employment was only associated to delinquency among the most economically disadvantaged. If, as Haurin's findings imply, minority youths do suffer more from having a working mother, it may be an indication that working conditions are a more powerful influence on juvenile behavior because minority youth are more likely to have mothers who work in low-status positions (Haurin 1992).

In general, it may be hypothesized that race shapes the effects of maternal employment to the extent that racial minorities are more likely to occupy jobs that are low in complexity, autonomy, and stability. Among working mothers and their children, then, Blacks and Hispanics may have more strained relations in the home due to the lower quality of jobs they are likely to hold. On the other hand, because race is highly related to family income, minority children may benefit, on average, from maternal employment if the alternative is poverty or welfare. In other words, children are likely to gain advantages from maternal employment if it significantly improves their economic conditions, but the benefits of maternal employment will diminish as working conditions decline.

Family Structure, Maternal Employment, and Delinquency

Another potential influence on the impact of maternal work is family structure. A study by Wadsworth (1979) showed that the negative effects of maternal employment were largely attributable to differences in family structure. The author showed that a large portion of the working mothers in his sample had experienced a marital break-up early in the study child's life and suspected that behavioral problems in the children of working mothers could just as easily be explained by family disruption. Although he found that early maternal work (when children were between 0 and 6 years old) was associated with later delinquency, this relationship disappeared after controlling for permanent family break-up, family size, and crowdedness in the home. Similarly, Parcel and Menaghan (1994) found that children of working mothers were more likely to have behavioral problems if their mothers had experienced the dissolution of a marriage or if they were stably single.

Recent work by Menaghan et al. (1997) lends additional support to the idea that the effects of maternal work are influenced by family structure. The authors found that increasing occupational complexity lowered the behavioral problems of the children of single mothers but had no significant effects on the children in other types of families. This finding suggests that higher quality maternal work not only improves the financial circumstances of female-headed families, but may also be related to maternal functioning and parent-child relations.

Unmarried mothers and divorced mothers not only often experience economic adversity but also are also potentially faced with performing parenting duties alone. When working mothers have a spouse or partner who is involved in parenting, maternal stress may be lower and mother-child relations may be of a higher quality. Conversely, divorced working mothers may find their parenting responsibilities even more challenging. Divorce has been found to be one of life's most stressful events (Amato 1993), and the fact that divorced mothers have less social support than married ones (Weinraub and Wolf 1983) means that children of divorce are often raised by highly distressed primary caregivers who are without a strong support system.

The marital status of working mothers is relevant because single working mothers might face additional hardships due to economic strain, role overload, and a diminished level of social support. In general, past research has shown that being raised in an intact (two-parent) family has a positive effect on outcomes for children (Blankenhorn 1995; McLanahan and Booth 1989), especially among Whites (Haurin 1992; Thomas, Farrell, and Barnes 1996), and, in particular, that it decreases the probability of delinquent involvement (Dornbusch, Carlsmith, Bushwall, Ritter, Leiderman, Hastorf, and Gross 1985; Rankin and Kern 1994; Thomas, Farrell and Barnes 1996). In their meta-analysis of the relationship between "broken homes" and delinquency, Wells and Rankin (1991) found that the prevalence of delinquency in broken homes was 10-15% higher than in intact homes.

Single or divorced working mothers are potentially at a disadvantage because there is one less adult present to support and supervise the children. Also, single-parent families may be prone toward producing conduct-disordered or delinquent children because such families are more likely to live in poverty (Mednick 1994), which is related to strained family relations, ineffective parenting, and antisocial behavior in children (McLeod, Kruttschnitt, and Dornfeld 1994).

Family disruption and mother's employment are interconnected in other ways. Hetherington (1981) explained that divorce can result in mothers entering the workforce, often in the form of low-paying or part-time jobs that result in diminished time spent with children. Additionally, divorced mothers who are drawn away from their children by erratic work schedules may overcompensate for lost time by being "ineffectually authoritarian in dealing with children" (see Hetherington 1981). Furthermore, through maternal employment and task overload the child may feel maternally deprived rather than paternally deprived as the custodial mother tries to distribute her energies across a larger range of roles (Hetherington 1981).

Family structure (e.g., intact vs. single-mother families) is likely to contribute to the working mother's adaptation to a wide range of role responsibilities. What may be more critical to family functioning, however, is the actual quantity and quality of father involvement in housework and child care. Hoffman (1983) found that highly involved fathers eased the role strain felt by working mothers, which improved familial relations and child outcomes. When children reside with their biological fathers, there is little doubt that a stable father-child relationship is beneficial to the child in a variety of ways. Highly involved fathers contribute directly to the cognitive and emotional development of their children and are more likely to have high marital quality, which contributes substantially to child development (see Furstenberg 1994).

There is much controversy over the benefits of the relationship between the noncustodial father and his children. Some studies demonstrate that children, in general, are better off by having frequent contact with their non-custodial fathers (see Blankenhorn 1995). Other studies, however, have found no differences in child outcomes based on father contact. (Furstenberg and Cherlin 1991; King 1994). The key to understanding the effects of contact between non-custodial fathers and children is a recognition that marital dissolution is often followed by continuing parental conflict. Parental conflict is detrimental to children, in both intact and broken families, and may have an enhanced effect on children when contact with the father is high (Furstenberg and Cherlin 1991).

Whether the father lives with his child or not, he may ease the burdens of a working mother by helping with child care, supervising and monitoring his children, and supporting the child both emotionally and financially. An involved father, custodial or otherwise, should help to insulate the children of working mothers against some of the delinquent pressures that they endure. In light of the expansive research on the contributions of involved spouses and fathers, it is critical to examine the relationship between maternal work and relationship within the context of family structure, as well as the links between mother's work, family processes, and delinquency within single-mother and married-mother sub-groups.

Another potential influence on the relationship between maternal work and child outcomes is the neighborhood context. Welfare reliance, for example, may be associated with delinquency because welfare-reliant families are most likely to live in economically-depressed, high-crime communities. Neighborhood effects have only been investigated in one study related to maternal employment and delinquency. In that study, Roy (1963) found that children living in urban settings were more likely to be delinquent if their mothers worked full-time, but found no such relationship among rural children. Roy (1963) explained this difference by arguing that there is an increased need for rural children to perform household chores when their mothers work. He argued that rural children experience higher levels of control on their behavior because their after-school time is more likely to be filled with farm work or other domestic household functions.

An alternative explanation for the differences between urban and rural effects is that urban children live in more socially disorganized, higher crime areas than rural children and thus are more likely to be exposed to criminal opportunities and delinquent peers. Roy's (1963) findings hint that neighborhood effects may influence the relationship between mother's work and delinquency. Accordingly, this analysis introduces neighborhood characteristics as a control in the present analysis because the residential setting may offer differential opportunities and constraints on the behaviors of the children of employed mothers.

Gender, Maternal Employment, and Delinquency

An important issue omitted by past researchers is the possibility that maternal work affects the behaviors of male and female children differently. This is a significant research question because gender is one of the most powerful predictors of delinquent involvement. Males are much more likely than females to be involved in most forms of delinquent behavior (Belknap 1996; Canter 1982; Cernkovich and Giordano 1987; Hindelang 1971; Johnson 1986; Van Voorhis, Cullen, Mathers, and Garner 1988). Some scholars have found that gender differences in delinquent involvement can be traced to gender differences in the ways that sons and daughters are controlled and socialized by parents. For example, female adolescents generally receive more parental supervision than males (Cernkovich and Giordano 1987; Hagan et al. 1985; Van Voorhis et al. 1988).

Although there are no clear patterns in the delinquency literature, it appears that some family functions may be gender-specific in the way they protect children from delinquent influences. Cernkovich and Giordano (1987) found that family variables have predictive power in explaining both male and female delinquency, but that different family dimensions have varying effects depending on gender. The authors found that variables related to control and supervision were more critical for males, while family support functions (e.g., identity support, parental disapproval of peers) were more important for females (1997). In similar findings, Simpson and Elis (1994) found parental attachment (a form of control) to be more critical for boys in reducing delinquency and Van Voorhis et al. (1988) discovered a gender-family interaction in their sample, with home quality having a greater effect on delinquency in females than in males.

Family structure also has been seen to shape delinquency differently for boys and girls. Johnson (1986) found that self-reported delinquency in males was highest when youths lived with a natural mother and a stepfather, while officially delinquent girls were most commonly found in mother-only homes.

If maternal employment has a gendered effect on the ways in which mothers and their children interact, we should expect gender differences in the delinquent outcomes of such children. It may be that sons are more vulnerable to the effects of maternal employment if control and supervision are compromised in the process. Girls may actually have a lower probability of delinquent involvement if working mothers are more likely to provide them with identity support and self-confidence, which should raise school attachment and achievement and thus lower delinquency. Evidence from the maternal employment literature suggests that daughters do benefit more than males from maternal employment and that those benefits may translate into lower delinquency rates.

Sons and daughters have been found to experience their mother's employment status differently. In her review of sex differences in the effects of maternal employment in children, Hoffman (1989) reported that daughters appear to fare better than sons when mothers are employed. Daughters tend to have more secure attachments to their mothers and less anxiety than male children (Belsky and Rovine 1988; Goldberg and Easterbrooks 1988), and thus tend to develop less stereotyped views of sex roles, which is more important for the self-esteem of young girls (Hoffman 1989). Additionally, others have found that maternal employment is related to increased cognitive performance in girls (Gottfried, Gottfried, and Bathurst 1988; Mott 1991).

These gender differences may be partially explained by the way in which mother's employment affects the mother-child relationship. Investigators have demonstrated that working mothers show more positive involvement with daughters than sons (see Bayder and Brooks-Gunn 1991; Zaslow, Pederson, Suwalsky, Cain, and Fivel 1985). Conversely, unemployed mothers are more positively involved with sons than daughters (Zaslow et al. 1985).

Finally, boys of employed mothers have been found to be more defiant than boys of unemployed mothers or girls of employed mothers (Crockenberg and Litman 1991). Given the known gender differences, it appears that maternal employment generally, and stressful employment specifically, could produce delinquent risk factors in boys such as insecure attachment, poor parental relations, and conduct disorder in childhood. For girls, the opposite may be true. Working mothers may, in fact, insulate their daughters against delinquent pressures. I will attend to these issues in this study by investigating the connection between maternal employment and delinquency in male and female sub-groups.

The above review of past research on maternal employment and delinquency illuminates some of the unresolved issues that will be addressed in this study. Specifically, past investigators imply that further research must focus on the differential effects of maternal employment and delinquency that occur in different subgroups. I will address these issues by examining the manner in which family structure interacts with maternal work to affect outcomes. Additionally previous work has shown that the emphasis on social control mechanisms (e.g., supervision and attachment) has failed to fully explain the relationship between maternal employment and delinquency. Other intervening variables, such as parental discipline style, parental support, family conflict, and school attachment deserve consideration. In the following section, I discuss in detail the intervening variables or "pathway" variables that I will include in the present analysis.

Mother's Work and Pathways to Delinquency

Over the last two decades, social scientists have produced an expansive body of research findings on the impact of maternal employment on outcomes for children. Maternal employment researchers have found that mother's work, in and of itself, does not have a significant negative effect on the children of working mothers (Barling 1990; Greenstein 1993; Hoffman 1989; Silverstein 1991). Although it is true that the research findings in this area have been mixed, it is misleading to say that investigators have failed to find links between maternal employment and negative child outcomes.

The study of maternal employment and its effects has advanced far beyond simple comparisons between mothers who work outside the home and those occupied as full-time homemakers. Research in this area has employed increasingly elaborate models that include variables representing a broad variety of contextual factors (Parcel and Menaghan 1994). For example, in a review of the work on the effects of maternal employment, Hoffman (1989) found that the influence of maternal employment was dependent upon, among other things, parental attitudes and self-concept, the number of hours an employed mother worked, variable levels of social support, and the age and gender of the child.

Researchers have explored the impact of maternal employment on child outcomes across many developmental measures. Much of the research in this area is critical to understanding any possible link between mother's employment and delinquency because certain outcomes related to maternal employment may be associated with delinquency risk factors. In the following section, I will review the relevant literature on maternal employment and outcomes for children. I will offer interpretations of how these findings might relate to the study of mother's employment and delinquency by considering the findings in terms of some of the "known" pathways to delinquency.

The number of hours mothers spend in the workplace may determine differential outcomes for children. The critical question here is whether the amount of time spent in external employment is related to the amount of time and quality of time spent with children. It is important to know, for example, whether mothers who work overtime hours spend much less time on average with their children or if overtime hours are associated with highly-stressed mothers, which negatively influences interaction with children. Furthermore, if number of hours spent working outside the home is related to less time spent in childrearing activity, we need to know if the child of a working mother is adversely affected by being deprived of his or her mother's supervision, support, or involvement during her absence.

Generally, research into the effects of maternal employment shows that negative child outcomes are more probable as mother's work hours increase (Hoffman 1989). Parcel and Menaghan (1990, 1994) have found, however, a nonlinear relationship between hours of maternal employment and behavior in children. The authors point out that low parental work hours may produce stress and anxiety in parents, which may negatively affect a parent-child relationship. Additionally, low work hours may be associated with low household earnings could lower the overall quality of life for children.

Criminological theory suggests that as working hours increase, a child may be exposed to delinquency risk factors because prolonged absence of one's mother may involve: a weakening of mother-child attachment (Hirschi 1969), a decrease in the amount of expressive or instrumental support offered to children (Cullen 1994), an increase in the time a child spends associating with delinquent peers (Sutherland 1939), or a decrease in cognitive development, which could lead to delinquency risks, such as school failure (Agnew 1992). These theoretical predictions will be elaborated in the next section, where I report some of the relevant findings on mother's employment and outcomes for children within the contexts of theories of crime and delinquency

Mother's Employment and Supervision

Wells and Rankin (1988) argue that researchers have neglected to test the potential effects of direct parental control (e.g., parental supervision, monitoring) on delinquency. Instead, investigators have relied upon social control models where parental influence is generally regarded as an indirect, internalized force that guides the behavior of children who are more firmly bonded to parents. When direct controls have been tested as predictors of delinquency, researchers have usually focused on disciplinary styles and levels of monitoring or supervision of children's behavior.

The effects of low supervision on delinquent involvement are well established. Wells and Rankin (1988) found parental regulation, a variation on supervision, to be a significant correlate of delinquency, as have most others who have sought to explore the relative importance of supervision in predicting delinquency (Cernkovich and Giordano 1987; Hagan, Gillis, and Simpson 1985, 1987; Sampson and Laub 1993). In their meta-analysis of the effects of family factors on conduct disorder and delinquency, Loeber and Stouthamer-Loeber (1986) found low parental supervision to be one of the most powerful predictors of behavioral problems.

As previously stated, some criminologists have found that supervision of children is reduced when mothers are employed outside the home (e.g. Sampson and Laub 1993, 1994). This finding is reinforced, in part, by research generated by those who have looked for relationships between time spent in external employment and time spent with children. Demo (1992) claimed that non-employed mothers have roughly twice the amount of direct contact with their children as opposed to working mothers. Hoffman (1989) reported that mothers who worked more than twenty hours per week spent less time on average with infants and pre-school children. Similarly, others have found that involvement in paid employment inhibits the amount of time mothers spend directly supervising the activity of school-aged children (Montemayor 1984; Nock and Kingston 1984), especially during the hours directly following school when parents are at work (Muller 1995; Richards and Duckett 1994).

On the other hand, some researchers have found no effect (Paulson 1996) or positive effects of long maternal work hours on time spent with children. For instance, mothers employed full-time can compensate by spending more time with kids during nonwork hours and weekends (Easterbrooks and Goldberg 1985; Hoffman 1984). Also, an increasing time commitment to the workforce by mothers can result in fathers being more involved with children (Barnett and Baruch 1987; Pleck 1983; Richards and Duckett 1994), which could offset the decrease in maternal supervision.

Overall, the maternal employment literature suggests that time spent in external employment does negatively effect the amount of hours mothers spend with their children. As Hirschi (1969) has argued, however, direct parental supervision may be a weak predictor of adolescent deviance because "most delinquent acts require little time, and because most adolescents are frequently exposed to situations potentially definable as opportunities for delinquency" (1969, p. 88). A more important avenue to explore might be the extent to which maternal employment influences the kinds of peer associates children interact with during unsupervised periods. This possibility is discussed next within the context of differential association theory.

Mother's Employment and Delinquent Peer Association

Direct parental supervision requires the physical presence of one or both parents, which is likely to be related to parental time commitment to the workplace. A related issue is whether or not working mothers have less control over the kinds of personal associates with whom their children spend their unsupervised time. Keeping track of the social meanderings of adolescents may be hampered by work obligations.

This point is important because time spent with delinquent friends is one of the strongest predictors of delinquent behavior (Kercher 1988; Warr 1993). Sutherland's (1939) differential association theory of delinquency rests on the assumption that youths learn and practice delinquent behavior by associating with small, intimate peer groups that promote pro-criminal attitudes and beliefs. The theory predicts that a preponderance of pro-delinquent messages received, as opposed to anti-delinquent messages, will result in delinquent action. If the children of employed mothers spend more time on average in peer interaction and their peer relationships are less subject to parental review, we might find that differential association is an important variable connecting mother's work to child's delinquency. Research by Warr (1993) sheds some light on this possible relationship. Warr (1993) studied the coinciding existence of parental and peer influences on delinquent behavior and found that time spent with parents weakened and, in some cases, eliminated the influence of delinquent peers. It may be, then, that exposure to delinquent others is more compelling for children who spend more time away from their working mothers.

Little is known about the effect of mother's employment status on peer association. In the one known study related to maternal employment and peer interaction, Montemayor (1984) reported that teenaged boys spent less time with both parents and more time with peers when their mothers worked. Given the dearth of findings on this issue, an analysis of the extent to which work status is related to mother's knowledge of and control over her child's peer associations is needed. This issue will be examined in this study.

Mother's Employment and Attachment

Hirschi's social bond theory (1969) emphasizes the importance of strong informal bonds to parents, peers, and teachers in controlling deviant impulses in children. A variant of general social control perspectives, Hirschi's argument suggests that firmly bonded individuals are less likely to deviate from widely-held norms because deviation from those norms could result in sanctions that may threaten valued relationships. Children who are bonded or "attached" to their parents, then, have a higher "stake in conformity" (Colvin and Pauly 1983, p. 518), while the child who lacks a firm attachment to parents "does not care about the wishes and expectations of other people--that is, if he is insensitive to the opinion of others--then he is to that extent not bound by the norms. He is free to deviate" (Hirschi 1969).

Following Hirschi (1969), criminologists have included parent-child attachment in their explanatory models and found general support for the assumption that weak parent-child bonds are associated with delinquency (e.g., Gove and Crutchfield 1982; Loeber and Stouthamer-Loeber 1986; Sampson and Laub 1993). Few scholars, however, have investigated the role of structural variables in shaping parental attachment (Rosen 1985). One important exception to this omission can be found in the work of Sampson and Laub (1993), who found that residential mobility, family socioeconomic status, and family disruption were significantly related to attachment. They did not, however, discover an association between mother's employment and attachment. As previously argued, given the restrictiveness of the 1950s Gluecks' data employed by the authors, it is reasonable to believe that a new test of this relationship, with more expansive measures of mother's employment status, is in order.

Although parent-child attachment had been found to be critical to the development of coping skills and ego-resiliency in adolescence (Kobak and Sceery 1988), little is known about the potential effects of mother's time in the workforce and its impact on parental attachments among adolescents.

A large body of findings has been generated by researchers interested in early maternal employment and attachment in infants and pre-school children. The study results vary widely in this area. Some have found lower or weaker degrees of mother attachment among infants raised in nonparental care while mothers work (Barglow, Vaughn, and Molitor 1987; Belsky 1988; Belsky and Braungart 1991; Belsky and Rovine 1988; Stifter, Coulehan, and Fish 1993), more mother-avoidant behavior among infants of full-time working mothers (Schwartz 1983), and more anxiety about separation among kindergarten boys with working mothers (Goldberg and Easterbrooks 1988).

Others have found no direct relationship between time spent employed and the strength of the mother-child attachment (Chase-Lansdale and Owen 1987; Chira 1996; Easterbrooks and Goldberg 1988; Owen and Cox 1988; Owen et al 1984) or negative affective responses to nonparental care among children with too much or too little separation from mothers during the first year of life (Jacobson and Wille 1984).

Although research findings on the association between early maternal employment and attachment vary widely, there is ample reason to believe that maternal work may influence the bond between mother and child. Past research on this subject has been concerned with the degree to which the absence of working mothers results in decreased or insecure attachments. The focus, then, has been on maternal work hours. Another possibility is that working conditions, in addition to hours, are influential on child attachment. Stressful, inflexible, or coercive workplace conditions could affect parenting with negative consequences for attachment. This potential link between early maternal work and attachment will be investigated in the present study.

As for working mother-child attachment in adolescence, only one published study can shed light on the possible relationship. This report, which focused on the attachment phenomenon among a Mormon population, found that adolescents of unemployed mothers reported closer relationships with both parents (Mohan 1990). Given the paucity of information on the connection between maternal employment and mother-adolescent attachment, it is hard to make an informed prediction on potential outcomes. It might be argued that, generally, those mothers who spend more time with their adolescent children will have more opportunity to build a healthy attachment; because maternal employment is consistently related to decreased parental time involvement, it is fair to assume, then, that attachment might be inversely related to maternal work hours. Accordingly, this potential link may represent an avenue to delinquency and, thus, will be explored in this study.

Mother's Employment and Parental Support

Parental attachment is merely one of many informal controls that shields adolescents against delinquent influences. Attachment is not a simple linear product of parent-child interaction. Instead, feelings of attachment are born out of a complex system of support existing between parent and child that goes beyond direct control mechanisms such as supervision, monitoring, and discipline. Parents also guide the healthy development of children by sharing and discussing important issues with children and by taking an interest and actively participating in the activities of offspring.

Cullen (1994) has argued that the concept of social support has not received the explicit attention it deserves as an explanatory variable in criminological theory. Although the measurement of parental support has not been systematically integrated into delinquency models, Cullen (1994; Cullen and Wright 1997) has demonstrated the importance of this concept through his review of the scattered studies where dimensions of support figure prominently as delinquency predictors. For example, direct parental support (i.e., parental affection, the sharing of activities between parent and child, intimate communication) (Loeber and Stouthamer-Loeber 1986), perceived parental affection (Van Voorhis et al. 1988), and family cohesion (Farrell, Barnes and Banerjee 1995) all have been found to share an inverse relationship with delinquency.

Most recently, Wright (1996) has found that direct parental supports serve to reduce delinquency both directly and indirectly by buffering delinquent strains and improving the delivery of other types of direct controls. Furthermore, Wright (1996) found that parental supports are largely responsible for mediating the relationship between delinquency and critical structural variables such as family structure and income. These findings suggest that the path from maternal employment and delinquency may run through the supportive dimension of the mother-child relationship. Research on the relationship between mother's work and the amount and quality of support that she provides her children may offer some clues as to how this relationship works.

Most researchers interested in maternal employment and support for children have focused on infants and younger school-age children. This research has been pointed at the ways in which paid employment shapes parenting styles. Owen and Cox (1988) found that mothers who worked in excess of forty hours were less sensitive to the needs of their infants who, as a result, were anxious and dissatisfied during interaction with mothers. Others have discovered that role conflict related to maternal employment inhibits maternal responsiveness to children and results in less supportive parenting styles (Goldberg and Easterbrooks 1988; Greenberger and Goldberg 1989; MacEwen and Barling 1991).

In her review of research on maternal employment and the parent-adolescent relationship, Paulson (1996) cited studies where mother's work has been positively related to parent-child conflict and general tension in parent-child relations. In her own assessment of the impact of mother's work on support, however, no significant effects were found for responsiveness, encouragement, or praise offered to children. Similarly, Pett et al. (1994) found no negative effects of maternal employment on parental support and, in fact, found part-time employed mothers to be more supportive than full-time homemakers. Maternal working conditions have also been shown to affect parental styles. Menaghan et al. (1997) found that maternal employment was positively related to warmth and responsiveness and that warm and responsive parenting was more likely as occupational complexity increased.

One critical omission from this research is the extent to which maternal employment shapes the amount of instrumental, as opposed to expressive, support given to children. While expressive support refers to sending positive, affirming messages in the course of a relationship, instrumental support involves providing a child with the resources (money, information, guidance, skills) that he or she needs to reach a valued goal (Cullen 1994). Instrumental parental support could include helping a child with homework, being involved in a child's school activities, or providing an outlet for discussing important issues or problems. If maternal employment is associated -

-positively or negatively--with delinquency, it may be that it works through both expressive and instrumental support.

Mother's Employment and Parental Discipline

Discipline has been used to refer to a wide variety of parenting practices, such as physical punishment, love withdrawal, and scolding (Loeber and Stouthamer-Loeber 1986). In addition to referring to forms of punishment, discipline is also manifested in the structure of rules and the enforcement of rules that govern the behavior of children. The process of making and enforcing rules is often called "parental structuring" (e.g., Menaghan et al. 1997).

The relative importance of disciplinary forms and disciplinary structuring depends upon the age of children. Research has shown, for example, that physical discipline has a greater effect on infants and pre-school children while structuring is more critical for adolescents. Thus, when investigating the effects of early maternal employment (when children are less than three years old) on behavioral problems, one would emphasize physical punishment; and while looking at the effects of mother's current employment on delinquency, emphasize parental structuring.

Researchers have found that physical punishment can have negative effects on a variety of child outcomes. Steinmetz (1979), for example, presented a large body of evidence showing that the use of physical punishment on pre-school children was associated with later behavioral problems. Straus (1991), too, found that children who were spanked early in life were more likely to be involved in delinquency and crime later on.

Conversely, in their meta-analysis of the effects of various family factors on behavioral problems, Loeber and Stouthamer-Loeber (1986) did not find a strong association between physical punishment and conduct disorders and delinquency. The studies analyzed by Loeber and Stouthamer-Loeber (1986), however, were all focused upon adolescents and, as they argue, because physical punishment is used less frequently on older children, it becomes a less significant variable for this group. Because of the apparent age-dependent relationship between physical punishment and behavioral problems, this study investigated the relationship between early maternal employment, spanking, and behavioral problems.

Although little research has been done on maternal employment and the use of spanking, recent work by Giles-Sims, Straus, and Sugarman (1995) lends guidance as to the potential relationship. They found that the rate of spanking for 3 to 5-year-olds was highest for children living in poverty, for children in families receiving AFDC, and for those children who had mothers who were employed less than 40 weeks in the previous year. The authors argued that outside employment may increase economic stability and lower stress which reduce a child's risk of being spanked.

Furthermore, Giles-Sims et al. (1995) discovered that spanking was most frequent in the lowest socioeconomic group in the sample. This finding is consistent with research that has found higher rates of physical abuse of children among low-income populations (e.g., Gelles 1978). The authors stated that the relationship between class and spanking may be related to the types of jobs that parents hold; low-status jobs with little extrinsic and intrinsic rewards may be stressful and thus reduce parenting skills. This explanation is consistent with the results of Kohn's (1977) research, which found a greater probability of authoritarian parenting in lower-status occupational groups. Accordingly, the relationship between maternal job conditions and the use of spanking and whether or not this path leads to later behavioral problems are studied herein.

As previously argued, the use of physical punishment is much lower when children are adolescents (Straus 1991). By adolescence, parents are more likely to discipline children through parental structuring. Structuring involves employing and enforcing a set of rules to evoke conformity. Rules alone, however, do not result in conformity. Rules that are consistently applied and enforced are likely to reduce behavioral problems because children know that, if detected, a failure to abide by rules carries real consequences (Patterson 1982). Based on research by Menaghan et al. (1997), there is reason to believe that maternal employment is associated with the employment of a consistent set of rules for children. They found that mothers employed in more complex positions were more involved in parental structuring.

A related issue is whether or not children are allowed to participate in rule-making or in negotiating the enforcement of rules. In a review of the research on children's involvement in rule-making and child outcomes, Dornbusch (1989) demonstrated that child's involvement in decision-making has a non-linear effect on behavioral problems; that is, behavioral problems are highest when parents dominate the rule-making process or when children are responsible for making their own rules. Joint decision making, between parents and children, on the other hand, was associated with the lowest levels of behavior problems (Dornbusch 1989). It is probable that maternal working conditions have an effect on the extent to which mothers involve their children in the making of rules. Evidence of this relationship is implied in the work of Kohn (1977), who found that working-class mothers were most likely to be authoritarian and inflexible with children while middle-class mothers were more likely to negotiate household rules with children.

Maternal Employment and Family Conflict

Dating back to the 19th century, delinquency scholars have consistently looked to the "broken home"--families disrupted by marital dissolution or parental absence--as one of the dominant explanations for delinquency (Wells and Rankin 1991). Although this line of inquiry has resulted in a large accumulation of studies, the findings have been largely inconclusive.

Wells and Rankin (1991) attempted to bring clarity to this issue by performing a meta-analysis of 50 "broken homes" studies. They concluded that broken homes had a consistent and real pattern of association with delinquency; the prevalence of delinquency in broken homes was found to be 10-15% higher than in intact homes. While the Wells and Rankin study (1991) adds to our general understanding of the relationship between family structure and delinquency, it does not attempt to explain the causal process.

The "broken home" might affect child outcomes in a variety of ways. A divorce, for example, might result in the prolonged separation of a child from one of his or her parents. In the case of divorce, children are more likely to be separated from fathers. As discussed earlier, while many studies have found that children benefit from paternal involvement after divorce, just as many studies have found that the frequency of involvement with divorced fathers is not related to child adjustment (Simons, Whitbeck, Beaman, and Conger 1994). King (1994) has suggested that frequent child involvement with divorced fathers may carry negative effects because involved ex-spouses are forced to interact more in order to plan and facilitate visitation. Increased involvement between ex-partners may result in greater inter-parental conflict, which could counteract the benefits of father involvement.

Other researchers have found that parental conflict, rather than parental separation, is a more powerful link between family disruption and child behavior. Loeber and Stouthamer-Loeber (1986), for instance, found that marital discord, especially overt fighting between parents, is a stronger predictor of delinquency than parental separation. This finding is supported by studies that have found comparable levels of child behavior problems between children from unhappy marriages and children from broken homes (Loeber and Stouthamer-Loeber 1986). Furthermore, there is consistent evidence that children in high-conflict, intact families show more behavioral problems than children in low-conflict, one-parent families (see Tschann, Johnston, Kline, and Wallerstein 1989).

Parental conflict may contribute to child behavior problems in several different ways. Loeber and Stouthamer-Loeber (1986) suggest that children may suffer emotionally as a result of witnessing parental discord. Observing fighting between parents may result in emotional scars as well as serving as an anti-social model of conflict resolution. Additional research shows that marital strife may lower the quality of parenting. Unhappily married mothers are less likely to supervise children and more likely to hold negative attitudes towards children. It may be, then, that parental conflict contributes to delinquency only indirectly through its effect on parenting.

The impact of parental conflict is relevant to the present study because it is a potential pathway between mother's work and delinquency. According to Rogers (1996), there are two broad theoretical perspectives that offer alternative predictions for the relationship between maternal work and marital quality. First, the role-strain perspective would predict a negative association between maternal employment and marital quality. Maternal work would be expected to lower marital quality and raise conflict because employment may decrease the time partners spend together, because work demands may enhance intrapersonal stress, and because having to do the lion's share of domestic labor within the home may enhance feeling of marital inequity among working mothers (see Rogers 1996).

Opposing predictions spring from the resources perspective. The resources perspective would predict that maternal employment is positively related with marital quality because maternal employment is positively associated with life satisfaction in women (Hoffman 1989), because maternal employment can reduce economic strain, and because greater economic resources increase a wife's power in the marriage (see Rogers 1996).

In her own research, Rogers (1996) found some support for both the role-strain and resources perspectives. For continuously married families, she found that full-time work was associated with more marital conflict, especially as family size increased. This result is consistent with the role-strain predictions because it suggests that work demands create more conflict when parental responsibilities are greater. It also points to the importance of family structure--in this case family size--as an influence on the effects of maternal employment on outcomes.

On the other hand, Rogers's (1996) results for mother-stepfather families gave support to the resources perspective. Specifically, she discovered that full-time employment was associated with lower marital conflict as family size increased. Rogers argued that remarried mothers who bring children into the new relationship would feel more pressure to contribute to a family's finances. When mothers in such families do not contribute substantially to family finances, it may breed resentment in stepfathers who might wonder why they are obligated to support someone else's children. This explanation is consistent with the resources perspective because it argues that marital quality is enhanced when mother's employment helps to meet increasing financial needs (i.e., when family size is greater). Furthermore, Rogers's results regarding mother-stepfather families indicate once again that family structure (continuously married versus remarried) may influence the effects of maternal work on family outcomes.

While Rogers (1996) developed evidence regarding the association between maternal work hours and marital conflict, she did not consider the effects of maternal working conditions on marital quality. Because stressful and unsatisfying work is known to negatively influence marital relations (e.g., Pearlin and McCall 1990), this research examines the relationship between occupational class, marital conflict, and associated behavioral problems.

Mother's Work and School Attachment

Criminologists have consistently found that school failure (Agnew and White 1992; Hirschi 1969; Kercher 1988; Loeber and Dishion 1983; Thornberry, Moore and Christenson 1985) and low school attachment (Hirschi 1969; Kercher 1988; Sampson and Laub 1993) are related strongly to later delinquency. There is some question, however, as to how school experiences and delinquency are connected. Agnew and White (1992) and Thornberry, Moore, and Christensen (1985) point out that school failure could be taken as either a measure of strain or of social control. Within the logic of Agnew's General Strain theory of crime and delinquency (Agnew 1992; Agnew and White 1992), school failure, such as low grades, could be construed as strain because they represent an interference with "the achievement of respondent's goals...have been associated with other noxious stimuli... or represent the removal of positive stimuli (for those who previously had high grades)" (Agnew and White 1992, p.481). Because such strains produce negative affective states in individuals, delinquency may follow.

On the other hand, school failure may represent a weakening in social control over the individual because negative experiences in school may be followed by an erosion of commitment or attachment to formal education, which effectively "frees the adolescent to engage in delinquency and drug use" (Agnew and White 1992, p. 476). When testing for the effects of schooling on delinquency, then, separate measures for failure and attachment should be obtained in order to capture both the strains and controls associated with school experiences.

In their attempt to model structural effects on family process and child development variables, Sampson and Laub (1993) did not find a significant relationship between maternal work hours and school achievement but did detect an inverse relationship between mother's work and school attachment. As discussed above, given the age and nature of the Gluecks' data, this potential relationship deserves further attention.

Maternal employment might lead to delinquency in children if it affects the quality or quantity of time that mothers spend with their children. If hours worked lowers the amount of time mothers spend helping children with homework, supervising after-school leisure time, or participating in school activities, then we might see a related decrease in school performance or attachment. This is a reasonable assumption because parental involvement in the education of children is an established predictor of performance in school (see Muller 1995).

Conversely, paid employment may benefit the children of working mothers when women hold positions that are high in complexity, which should enhance the level of cognitive stimulation received by children in the home. Parcel, Nickoll, and Dufur (1996) showed that reading achievement in children was especially high when their mothers had complex work <u>and</u> worked part-time hours; seemingly, stimulating work experiences are most effectively translated into stimulating parenting when mothers have additional time to spend with children.

Recently, Parcel, Nickoll, and Dufur (1996) found no significant cognitive advantages for children of unemployed mothers. Some researchers have found, however, that full-time maternal employment can have negative effects on general cognitive achievement and school performance (e.g., Banducci 1967; Milne et al. 1986). Maternal employment in the first year of life has been associated with lower cognitive achievement among three year olds (Baydar and Brooks-Gunn 1991), while school grades and cognitive ability were adversely affected when mothers increased work hours from part time to full time (Moorehouse 1991). Longer work hours have similarly been related to lower math achievement (Muller 1995) and to weaker verbal facility (Parcel and Menaghan 1990) in children.

Others have discovered a positive relationship between working mothers and various achievement measures in their children (e.g., Hoffman 1989; Parcel and Menaghan 1994; Vandell and Ramanan 1992) or no significant relationship at all between mother's employment status and measures of cognitive development in children (Blau and Grossberg 1990; Gottfried, Gottfried, and Bathurst 1988; Heyns 1982; Heyns and Catsambis 1985).

Given the mixed findings on this issue, it appears that the relationship between maternal employment and school performance and attachment is still unclear. If mother's work reduces time spent helping children with homework and attending school activities, we should expect a corresponding negative effect on school performance and attachment. Furthermore, it may be that the process has more to do with quality of time spent with children rather than quantity. If this is the case, maternal work hours should only be a weak predictor at best. A stronger influence on school attachment may be mother's working conditions, which may affect maternal stress and, consequently, the child's school achievement and attachment. Unfortunately, the NLSY data do not contain a strong measurement of school achievement. However, the effects of mother's work on school attachment are assessed.

The next chapter includes discussions of the study sample and methodological approach.

CHAPTER TWO

Exploring the National Longitudinal Survey of Youth

In the 1960s, the United States Department of Labor hired the Center for Human Resource Research at Ohio State University to gather longitudinal data on the labor market experiences of four representative target groups among the U.S. population (Fahey 1995). A fifth cohort of men and women between the ages of 14 and 22 was identified in 1979. Known as the National Longitudinal Survey of Youth (NLSY), this project involved a multistage stratified random sampling that produced 12,686 subjects, 11,404 of whom were interviewed annually about their occupational, educational, familial, and childbearing experiences (see Chase-Lansdale, Mott, Brooks-Gunn, and Phillips 1991; Parcel and Menaghan 1994).

In 1986, the NLSY began supplementing the youth data by giving a variety of developmental assessments that measure cognitive ability, motor and social development, and behavior problems and home environment to the cohort of children born to the women in the original sample. This cohort, known as the Children of the NLSY, originally contained over 90 percent of the 5,236 children born to sample mothers. The great majority of these offspring were re-assessed in 1988, 1990, and 1992.

By 1994, 10,042 children of sample mothers were identified to report on their home environment, family relations, and school experiences in addition to taking a number of inventories designed to measure cognitive and socioemotional development. After selecting out children born to sample dropouts and excluding those who no longer live in their mother's home, 7,089 children were assessed in 1994 (Users Guide 1997). By matching these child data with the corresponding information gathered from NLSY mothers, researchers have been able to investigate over time the family processes of an unprecedented number of parent-child pairs (Chase-Lansdale et al. 1991).

Sample

To investigate the relationship between maternal work and delinquency, I conducted my analysis on a sample of 707 adolescents who were between the ages of 12 and 14 in 1994. These children are the offspring of female respondents originally interviewed in 1979. Because these women were interviewed annually since 1979, data on maternal work experiences, maternal psychological functioning, and childrearing practices are available for the fifteen years leading up to and including 1994. For the current analysis, I focus on the 707 children who completed the Child Self-Administered Supplement (CSAS). This self-report booklet collects information on a wide range of variables including child-parent interaction, peer relationships, and involvement in various delinquent activities.

Additionally, the children of the NLSY mothers were studied every other year beginning in 1986, so data on various developmental outcomes are available from early childhood up through early and middle adolescence for this sample. To study the effects of both early and current maternal employment on delinquency, I will follow this sample from 1994 back to 1986 when study children were between the ages of 4 and 6 years old. I selected 1986 as the study year for early employment effects because it was the first year that NLSY researchers collected extensive data on parent-child interaction and family relations.

Because my theoretical model predicts that early employment operates through family processes to influence delinquency, I must measure these variables and early employment at or around the same time period. That is, the delinquency pathways should be measured soon after the period of employment that is hypothesized to be the causal influence. Thus, I measure early employment and delinquency pathways in 1986.

Other investigators have studied this period of early childhood (from 2 years to 6 years of age) to examine the influence of various environmental factors and family arrangements on child outcomes. Parcel and Menaghan (1994), for example, consistently found that parental employment conditions when children were between the ages of 3 and 6 influenced cognitive and social outcomes measured two years later.

The significance of early childhood events has long been a focus of developmental psychologists, who have produced evidence that early childhood experiences can affect a wide range of outcomes in adolescence (see Rutter 1988). The early childhood years are especially critical for establishing pro-social behavioral patterns and norms because these are the years when children begin to struggle for a sense of autonomy while maintaining a strong bond with parents at the same time (Erikson 1959).

Two- to six year-olds also develop relatively enduring patterns of behavior that have been shown to be good predictors of behavior in adolescence (Benson 2002). Fischer, Rolf, Hasazi, and Cummings (1988), for example, found that conduct-disordered 2-6 year-olds were almost three times as likely to have behavior problems seven years later. This finding is important to the present study because I will be investigating the impact of early employment on later delinquency through early risk factors.

Like developmental psychologists, criminologists have sometimes focused on early childhood experiences to explain variations in delinquent involvement in adolescence. Among the more notable findings in this literature, researchers have found that adolescent behavior problems are directly related to social and economic deprivation at age five (Kolvin, Miller, Fleeting, and Kolvin 1988), to family functioning at age six (Craig and Glick 1963), to SES at age four (Wadsworth 1979), to family size at age two (Wadsworth 1979), and to home environment at age five (McCord 1979).

Linking early childhood experiences to adolescent outcomes is a difficult task. The temporal distance between any given childhood experience or status, such as maternal employment or child care, and an adolescent outcome is significant (Baker and Mednick 1981). When performing this type of research, the investigator must be aware that any association found between early experiences and later outcomes may be explained by influences that occurred in the intervening period. To avoid making this type of error, researchers must introduce statistical controls that represent events or statuses in the intervening period. Often, researchers have interpreted the effects of early experiences without controlling for concurrent effects of the causal variable in question. Belsky and Eggebeen (1991), for example, investigated the effects of early maternal employment on behavior problems in school without controlling for current employment.

I take advantage of the longitudinal nature of the NLSY data by controlling for 1994 employment when examining the effects of 1986 employment on 1994 delinquency. By controlling for current employment, I will lend support to any assertions that the effect of early employment is independent of the effect of current employment.

To investigate the effects of current maternal employment, I will measure mother's employment and delinquency pathways in 1992 and delinquency in 1994. Measuring parental supervision in 1992, for instance, makes sense because it will represent a level of parental monitoring that took place before the delinquency measured in 1994. If I measured supervision in 1994, on the other hand, it would be difficult to untangle the causal order of parental supervision and child behavior since each might have direct impact on the other. Finally, because mothers might have left or changed jobs in between the two periods of measurement (1992 and 1994), I control for change of employment in 1993.

It should be apparent that the advantages of working with longitudinal data are tempered somewhat by the difficulties of capturing theoretical concepts in a temporally logical manner. The NLSY data, while presenting great possibilities for research, have their shortcomings. One limitation of these data, for example, is that the Children of the NLSY are not a nationally representative group. Over 27 percent of the 707 children who were between the ages of 12 and 14 in 1994 were born to mothers who were less than twenty years old when they gave birth to their children. As a result, many of these mothers are less-educated and are more likely to be members of a minority group than one would find in a representative sample where maternal age is normally distributed (Chase-Lansdale et al. 1991). Because early child bearers are more prone to having children with developmental deficits, such as low cognitive ability (Luster and McAdoo 1994) and are at a greater risk for criminality (e.g., Morash and Rucker 1989), these children should be considered to be a high-risk group.

This problem can be dealt with in one of two ways. First, some researchers have weighted the data to correct for the large number of lower socio-economic and minority women in the sample (e.g., Parcel and Menaghan 1994). NLSY data managers strongly suggest that the urge to use a weighted analysis be resisted. According to the NLSY Users Guide (1997), using weighted data is potentially problematic because the composition of the sample can change in subtle ways depending upon which respondents were interviewed in any given year. Weighting the data, then, may potentially misrepresent the actual distribution of ethnic and racial members across years.

A second way to deal with the uniqueness of this population is to make inferences only to this segment of the population when interpreting findings, noting that child outcomes were achieved in a high-risk environment. One advantage of studying this relatively disadvantaged sample is that this group of women and children may closely resemble the population that is most often focused on for public policy intervention (King 1994). This approach is followed using unweighted data, while noting that generalizability to older and more advantaged mothers may be limited. As Menaghan et al. (1997) argue, older mothers tend to have greater resources (e.g., education, cognitive ability) that increase resilience to social stressors such as employment. To give further support to the findings, maternal resources are controlled in all regression models. The focus is primarily on the unweighted data, although it will be run against the weighted data to see if the results differ. The sample characteristics and the variables used in the analysis are described below. The analytic strategy employed to investigate the impact of maternal employment is also highlighted. The sample characteristics and the variables used in the analysis are described below.

Sample Characteristics

Table 1 lists the demographic characteristics of the sample used in the analysis. The mean age of study children is 13.27 years, approximately half of the sample is female. Thirty-five percent of this sample is White, 44 percent African-American, and 19 % Latino. Sample mothers average just under 12 years of education (i.e., less than a high school diploma). Fifty-four percent of sample mothers reported working in the paid labor market in 1992.

Table 1. Sample Characteristics.

Variable	Mean	SD	Response Range Min.	Max.
Child Characteristics				
Age	13.27	.74	12.00	14.75
Female	.49	.50	.00	1.00
Race	.59	.49	.00	1.00
Maternal Characteristics				
AFQT	571.41	204.47	.00	1015.00
Education 1986	11.53	3.60	1.00	19.00
Education 1992	11.66	2.09	1.00	19.00
Intact Marriage 1986	.56	.49	.00	1.00
Intact Marriage 1992	.47	.49	.00	1.00
Maternal Employment				
Hours 1986	36.95	8.67	1.00	75.00
Hours 1992	37.92	8.31	3.00	96.00
Family Income 1986	18818.83	14373.43	.00	100001.
Family Income 1992	27664.02	16590.36	.00	100001.
Coercive Controls 1986	.19	.39	.00	1.00
Technical Controls 1986	.20	.40	.00	1.00
Bureaucratic Controls 1986	.07	.26	.00	1.00
Welfare 1986	.22	.41	.00	1.00
Coercive Controls 1992	.21	.41	.00	1.00

Table 1. (cont'd) Sample Characteristics.

Variable	Mean	SD	Response Range Min.	Max.
Technical Controls 1992	.20	.40	.00	1.00
Bureaucratic Controls 1992	.13	.34	.00	1.00
Welfare 1992	.17	.38	.00	1.00
Occupational Complexity 1986	.75	2.90	-6.51	8.86
Occupational Complexity 1992	.82	3.61	-15.94	10.05
Child Care				
Family Care	.22	.42	.00	1.00
Non-Family Private	.05	.23	.00	1.00
Professional Center	.24	.43	.00	1.00
Early Delinquency Pathways				
Insecure Attachment	19.48	4.35	9.00	35.00
Warmth and Responsiveness	2.72	1.11	.00	4.00
Spanking	1.96	3.30	.00	62.00
Current Delinquency Pathways				
Supervision	3.34	.90	1.00	4.00
Delinquent Peers	.35	1.00	.00	5.00
Warmth and Responsiveness	3.40	.94	.00	4.00

Table 1. (cont'd) Sample Characteristics.

Variable	Mean	SD	Response Range	
			Min.	Max.
Attachment	3.47	.79	.00	4.00
School Attachment	3.24	.90	1.00	4.00
Neighborhood Disorder	9.66	2.17	4.00	12.00
Delinquency Index	2.14	2.05	.00	9.00

Dependent Variable

The 1994 CSAS includes nine highly correlated items that relate to child deviance and delinquency. Respondents were asked to report on their involvement in a variety of behaviors over the last twelve months. If children reported that they had no involvement in any given act, that variable received a score of 0. If the respondent had been involved in that activity over the past year, the variable received a score of 1. Table 2 lists the variables used to construct a general delinquency index. The delinquency index has a reliability of .78.

This multiple-item measure is consistent with past research on delinquency in that it makes use of a range of self-reported delinquent acts to construct a general delinquency scale (Canter 1982; Elliott, Huizinga, and Ageton 1985). The self-reported nature of this data should be regarded as a suitable measure of true delinquent involvement for these acts because self-reports have consistently been found to be valid indicators of delinquency. Although chronic offenders who may be incarcerated are often missing from self-report samples

(Cernkovich, Giordano, and Pugh 1985) and the most serious acts may go unreported (Elliott and Huizinga 1989), the relationship between official reports and self-reports is consistently high (Elliott and Voss 1974; Hindelang, Hirschi, and Weis 1981; West and Farrington 1977). Recently, Farrington et al. (1996) demonstrated that self-reported delinquency has both predictive validity (self-reports predict future delinquency) and concurrent validity (self-reports compared to official reports). Furthermore, although Hindelang et al. (1981) discovered racial differences in the validity of self-reports, the more recent research by Farrington et al. (1996) found that self-reported delinquency has predictive and concurrent validity for all sample respondents regardless of race.

Finally, this measure of delinquency is skewed towards non-offending. Nearly 25 percent of the adolescent sample reported no involvement in any of the nine delinquency items used to create the scale. Furthermore, over 75 percent of the sample reported involvement in no more than three of the nine items used to construct the index. Efforts will be made to normalize this distribution for analysis. For example, I will construct a variable equal to the natural logarithm of the delinquency variable in order to increase the explainable variance in delinquency.

Independent Variables

Table 3 provides a detailed explanation of the independent pathway, and control variables used in the analysis.

Table 2. Delinquency Index.

Variable	Mean	SD	Description
Breaking Parents' Curfew	.51	.50	In the last year, have you broken curfew? 1 = yes, 0 = no
Dishonesty	.52	.50	In the last year, have you lied about something important? 1 = yes, 0 = no
School Problems	.27	.44	In the last year, have you had to bring your parents to school because of something you did wrong? 1 = yes, 0 = no
Truancy	.10	.30	In the last year, have you skipped a day of school without permission? 1 = yes, 0 = no
Out All Night	.15	.36	In the last year, have you stayed out at least one night without permission? 1 = yes, 0 = no
Alcohol Abuse	.09	.29	In the last year, have you gotten drunk? 1 = yes, 0 = no
Vandalism	.11	.31	In the last year, have you damaged school property on purpose? 1 = yes, 0 = no
Damaged Property	.17	.38	In the last year, have you damaged property of others on purpose? 1 = yes, 0 = no
Theft	.16	.36	In the last year, have you taken something from a store without paying for it? 1 = yes, 0 = no
Violence	.21	.41	In the last year, have you hurt someone badly enough to need bandages or a doctor? 1 = yes, 0 = no

Table 3. Maternal Work, Pathway Variables, and Control Variables (Alpha Reported).

Maternal Employment Measures	
Non-Employed	Non-employed mothers reported that they did not work for pay during the last week and did not receive AFDC in the last year.
Welfare-Reliant	Mothers who did not work for pay during the last week and received AFDC during the last year.
Work Hours	I dummied hours of work; for mothers, I designated low part-time workers (1-20 hours), High part-time workers (21-24 hours), full-time workers (35-40 hours) and overtime workers (over 40 hours). For fathers, I designated part-time workers (less than 35 hours), full-time workers (35-40 hours) and overtime workers (41 hours or more).
	A continuous work hours variable was also used. Non-working mothers and fathers were assigned the mean value for hours worked.
Occupational Class	This is a series of dummy variables representing the three fractions of the working class. Each mother and father, if present, was assigned a class fraction status (1, 2, 3) based upon the presumed skill-level, autonomy, and job stability of their listed occupation.
Pathway Variables	
Insecure Attachment 1986 (Alpha = .52)	Mothers were asked to report the usual behavioral tendencies of their child using a five-point scale. A response of 5 reflects a child who behaves like this most of the time: - trouble soothing or calming - stays close to mother during play - copies mother's behavior - cries when left alone - demanding and impatient when mother is busy - gets worried when mother is upset - needs help

Table 3. (Cont'd). Maternal Work, Pathway Variables, and Control Variables (Alpha Reported).

Supervision 1992	How often does your mother know who you are with when you're not home? 1 = often, 2 = sometimes, 3 = hardly ever
Delinquent Peer Association 1992 (Alpha = .79)	Do you ever feel pressure from your friends to do any of the following things? Try cigarettes? 1 = yes, 0 = no Try marijuana or other drugs? 1 = yes, 0 = no Drink alcohol? 1 = yes, 0 = no Skip school? 1 = yes, 0 = no Commit a crime or do something violent? 1 = yes, 0 = no
Maternal Support 1986 (Alpha = .79)	Did you (interviewer) observe mother speak spontaneously to her child twice or more? 1 = yes, 0 = no Mother responded verbally to child's speech (excluding scolding) 1 = yes, 0 = no Mother answered child's questions or requests verbally. 1 = yes, 0 = no Mother caressed, kissed or hugged child at least once. 1 = yes, 0 = no Mother introduced interviewer to child by name. 1 = yes, 0 = no Mother's voice conveyed positive feeling about child. 1 = yes, 0 = no
Maternal Support 1992 (Alpha = .76)	Did you (interviewer) observe mother encourage child to talk? 1 = yes, 0 = no Mother conversed with child (excluding scolding) 1 = yes, 0 = no Mother answered child's questions or requests verbally. 1 = yes, 0 = no Mother introduced interviewer to child by name. 1 = yes, 0 = no Mother's voice conveyed positive feeling about child. 1 = yes, 0 = no
Early Maternal Discipline	About how many times, if any, have you had to spank your child in the past week?

Table 3. (Cont'd). Maternal work, Pathway Variables, and Control Variables (Alpha Reported).

Adolescent Attachment	How close do you feel to your mother? 1=extremely close...4=not at all close
School Attachment	How satisfied are you with your school? 1=Very Dissatisfied 2=Somewhat Dissatisfied 3=Somewhat Satisfied 4=Very Satisfied

Marital Conflict (Alpha = .75)	How frequently do you and your (husband/partner) have arguments about: Chores and responsibilities? Your children? Money? Showing affection to each other? Religion? Leisure time? Drinking? Other women? His relatives? Your relatives? Score range: 0 = never, 1 = hardly ever, 2 = sometimes, 3 = often. Scores range from 0 to 30.

Control Variables	
Behavioral Problems (Index 1986) (Alpha = .90)	This consists of a 28-item scale drawn from mothers' reports of behavior problems.

Table 3. (Cont'd). Maternal Work, Pathway Variables, and Control Variables (Alpha Reported).

AFQT 1980	The AFQT consists of the sum of scores on four sub-tests of the Armed Services Vocational Aptitude battery.
Maternal Education	Measured as Mother's highest grade completed by survey year.
Neighborhood (Alpha = .85)	This scale is a summed construct of mother's responses to the following question: I'm going to read a list of problems that neighborhoods sometimes have. For each one, tell me if it is a big problem (1), somewhat of a problem (2), or not a problem (3). People don't have enough respect for rules and laws. Crime and violence Abandoned or run-down buildings Not enough police protection Too many parents who don't supervise their children People keep to themselves and don't care what goes on in the neighborhood Lots of people who can't find jobs
Age	Age of study child in years
Race	0 = Black or Hispanic; 1 = White
Sex	0 = Male and 1 = Female
Family Structure	0 = no marital partner in the home; 1 = mother is currently married and spouse is living in the home

Maternal Employment Status

Mother's work status is operationalized by a series of dummy variables that measure variation in hours spent in the paid workforce and welfare reliance. I drew this information from responses to the question, "How many hours did you work last week at all jobs?" Following Parcel and Menaghan (1994), I distinguished between low part-time hours (1-20), high part-time hours (21-34), full-time hours (35-40) and overtime hours (41 or more). The main purpose for employing the use of dummy variables versus measuring maternal employment hours continuously, is that dummied variables allow for the detection of nonlinearity between maternal employment and various outcomes. The current analysis was sensitive to the presence of nonlinearity because Parcel and Menaghan (1994) have found that maternal employment influenced certain child outcomes in a nonlinear fashion.

In past research (e.g., Parcel and Menaghan 1994), investigators have assigned missing values to work-hour variables for non-employed mothers. As a result, non-employed and welfare-reliant mothers were not included in the analysis. In contrast to past research, I assigned non-working mothers zero values for work hours. One of the main objectives of this study is to compare non-working mothers and welfare-reliant mothers to working mothers on various delinquency pathway and delinquency variables. In order to include welfare-reliant mothers, I employed the use of a dummy variable coded one if the respondent reported that she did not work during the survey week <u>and</u> if the respondent answered affirmatively to the question, "Did you or your spouse receive income from AFDC in the past calendar year?" In this way, I distinguished between those who draw income primarily from welfare and those who may draw welfare but participate in the workforce as well. Those who do not fit into the work-hours categories above are those who did not work in the survey week and did not draw welfare in the preceding year and, thus, make up the non-employed mothers category. These non-employed (not welfare-reliant) mothers represent the reference category or suppressor.

It is critical to differentiate welfare-reliant mothers from nonworking mothers who do not draw welfare, and from working mothers, to test for different effects on home environment and child outcomes. Recent work by Parcel (1996) suggests that welfare reliance, as opposed to paid work or unemployed, non-welfare status, has a unique and possibly deleterious effect on family processes and home environment. Furthermore, given current government efforts to shift welfare recipients into the workforce, it will be valuable to see if welfare-reliant mothers differ from mothers who hold low-status, low-paying jobs (the jobs many former welfare recipients will be competing for) with respect to family processes and delinquency in offspring.

A continuous measure of hours worked will also be used as an alternative to the series of dummy variables. As suggested by Menaghan et al. (1997), I ran models where dummy variables are employed to capture employment status (i.e., welfare, coercive, technical, and bureaucratic controls) while substituting mean values for the continuous variable measuring work-role conditions (i.e., hours worked) for non-working mothers. Regression estimates for the continuous hours variable reflect the effects for working mothers and coefficients for the occupational class dummy variables will "reflect the contrast between that group and the reference category, evaluated at average conditions on the continuous variables" (Menaghan et al. 1997).

When fathers are present in the home, I designated them as not-employed, part-time workers (less than 35 hours), full-time workers (35-40 hours), or over-time (41 or more hours). As with sample mothers, a continuous measure of father's work hours will also be used.

Occupational Class

Past researchers have employed various strategies to measure the content and conditions of occupations. Parcel and Menaghan (1994), for example, have constructed a 19-item-based occupational complexity scale by matching occupational titles reported by NLSY respondents to job descriptions reported in the *Dictionary of Occupational Titles*. The items that are used to create the scale include the extent to which individuals work with people versus things; measures of training and education required to perform the job; and direction and control of work activities. The occupational complexity scale used by Parcel and Menaghan (1994) is largely based upon the theory and research of Kohn and his colleagues (1977) who argue that occupational self-direction, autonomy, and complexity of job duties are critical in shaping the ways in which parents discipline, supervise, and support their children. A similar variable is created for this analysis.

Kohn's work also figures prominently in one of the few criminological theories that establishes a clear link between work, family life, and delinquency: Colvin and Pauly's "Structural Marxist" theory of delinquency production (1983). Colvin and Pauly drew from Kohn (1977) and Edwards (1979) to put forth a theory that links the workplace controls experienced by parents to the patterns and styles of control parents exert upon children. Colvin and Pauly argue that workers are more or less expendable due to the amount of training and technical skills they possess. As a result, unskilled, non-unionized employees (Fraction I workers) are subjected to "simple control" in the workplace that is coercive and alienating. Simple control involves exacting worker compliance through the threat of job termination. This type of control is then reproduced in the home through erratic, harsh, and punitive parenting. Children who are raised under these conditions may be likely to form an alienated bond with authority that frees them to behave in anti-social and delinquent ways.

Skilled laborers and craftspersons (Fraction II workers), who often belong to labor unions, experience greater job security and are controlled via "technical control." Technical control is accomplished through the machine-paced atmosphere of manufacturing and industrial workplaces where workers are motivated to produce by wage increases and job security. According to Colvin and Pauly (1983) workers who are controlled by "technical control" will be more likely to control their children through extending and suspending rewards and punishments which results in the formation of calculative bonds to authority in children. Such children are less likely be involved in serious delinquency than the children of Fraction I workers.

Fraction III workers are those skilled workers, technicians, salaried professionals, and supervisory staff who experience greater self-direction, job complexity, and job security in the workplace. Fraction III workers are controlled in a bureaucratic fashion which relies on the power of normative pressure to control workers. These workers are heavily invested in the rules of the organization due to their favored status and, as a result, tend to be self-regulating employees. Due to high levels of self-direction and autonomy in the workplace, Fraction III workers are positively bonded to authority which they reproduce in their children through a steady and consistent, normative family structure. Children of Fraction III workers are least likely to deviate from rules and laws due to their strong, normative bond with authority.

Tests of Colvin and Pauly's theory have produced mixed results with some evidence that workplace controls are related to parenting and delinquency in the manner in which the authors suggest (e.g., Messner and Krohn 1990; Simpson and Elis 1994). Empirical tests of the theory have been true to Colvin and Pauly's formulation by focusing on the compliance structures used by families and the kinds of bonds that children form towards authority. But this theory suggests a broader relationship between working conditions, parenting, and delinquency. Fraction I workers, for example, are not just alienated workers; we should also expect them to be less satisfied with their work, more highly stressed by their jobs, and generally more punitive and less supportive with their children as a result. The children of Fraction I workers, then, not only are likely to have alienated bonds, but are also more likely to be subjected to other delinquency risk factors such as ineffective discipline and unsupportive relationships. Furthermore, if Fraction I workers have coercive and stressful working conditions, it is also likely to affect other relationships, such as marriage. This suggests that working conditions, as represented by the three class fractions, may also influence delinquency through family conflict, a well-established predictor of delinquency.

Colvin and Pauly's class fraction scheme provides a simple and parsimonious method for linking general job conditions to family life and to delinquency. For that reason, I measured working conditions by assigning each NLSY mother an occupational class value. Occupational class is measured with a series of dummy variables representing the three class fractions of the working class. I made occupational class assignments based upon methods used by past researchers who have tested Colvin and Pauly's theory. First, using occupational codes in the NLSY data, I made an initial assessment about class fraction membership based on the presumed skill-level, autonomy, and job stability of each occupation (Messner and Krohn 1990). According to Colvin and Pauly, Fraction I workers are those unskilled, non-union workers found in agricultural labor, small-manufacturing firms, retail and food services, household domestic work, low-level clerical jobs (e.g., stock clerk) and sales (e.g., shoe sales, retail). All NLSY workers whose occupational titles fit the above description were placed in Fraction I. If a Fraction I worker reported union membership *and* job stability (no involuntary break in employment in the last twelve months), the worker was reassigned Fraction II status (Messner and Krohn 1990). Those assigned to Fraction II include skilled blue-collar workers (e.g., welders, plumbers, steel workers, and auto assemblers), skilled clerical workers (e.g., secretaries), craftsworkers, and low-level supervisors (e.g., foreman). Fraction III status was assigned to professionals, technicians, managers, government workers, and proprietors (Simpson and Ellis 1991).

When fathers were present in the household, they were assigned an occupational class status using the same process outlined above.

Wages

Following Parcel and Menaghan (1994), maternal wages were measured as the hourly rate of pay earned by working mothers. Wage levels for fathers were estimated by dividing total annual spouse earnings by the total number of spouse working hours. Non-working and welfare-reliant parents were assigned zero values for the wage variable. Total family income was used in all models as an alternative to maternal and paternal wages. The advantage of using family income over wages is that all mothers, working or not, can vary on family income. Furthermore, by employing the use of a family income measure, one can assess the impact of mother's employment experiences while controlling for the total standard of living of each family included in the analysis. Finally, past research suggests that family income may be a more important variable than wages in terms of its effect on family life and outcomes. Investigators have consistently found that family income has a significant positive effect on family processes and on child outcomes (e.g., McLeod, Kruttschnitt, and Dornfeld 1994).

Child Care

Following Parcel and Menaghan (1994), child care was measured with a series of dummy variables. Dummy variables representing commercial daycare settings, child care provided by a relative (including fathers), and child care provided by a non-relative were included.

Pathway Variables

Supervision

Supervision of children has been measured in a variety of ways. The Gluecks (1950) constructed an ordinal scale that rated children as receiving unsuitable, fair, or suitable supervision depending on whether mothers directly supervised the activities of their children or, failing that, arranged for other adults to monitor them. When addressing level of supervision, Wells and Rankin (1988) called their variable "regulation" which represents the extent to which parents decide the friends and activities of children. Another common operationalization of parental supervision is the degree to which parents know the whereabouts of children when they are away from home and who they are with when away from home (Aseltine 1995; Hagan, Gillis and Simpson 1990). I employ a similar measure of supervision found in the NLSY child self-administered supplement. My one-item measure is a four-point scale reflecting the child's report on how often "your mother knows who you are with when not at home."

Delinquent Peer Association

Differential association is generally captured through survey questions tapping into the number of delinquent friends possessed by the respondent. For example, exposure to pro-delinquent peers has been measured by the total number of close friends who have committed certain delinquent acts (Warr 1993), a ratio of total number of best friends to number of delinquent best friends (Johnson, Marcos, and Bahr (1987), and a 20-item scale that reflects the number of respondent's friends who have engaged in a variety of delinquent and drug-related acts (Agnew and White 1992). Johnson, Marcos, and Bahr (1987) argue that the differential association process should not be seen simply in terms of the kinds of people one associates with, but should also consider the *situational pressures* that go along with associating with certain types. The process, then, is best evaluated by gaining measures on the amount of pressure to be delinquent exerted by one's friends. The NLSY child self-administered supplement asked respondents to report on whether they felt pressure from friends to try cigarettes, try drugs, drink alcohol, skip school, or commit crime or do something violent. I combine these items into a differential association scale ranging from 0 to 5, with 5 being the highest degree of delinquent pressure. The reliability of this scale is .79.

Attachment

Attachment is often operationalized by items that relate to a child's feelings of closeness, love, or admiration for a parent. Following Hirschi (1969), many researchers have gauged attachment by determining the extent to which respondents want to be like their parent(s) (e.g., Hagan, Gillis, and Simpson 1990; Messner and Krohn 1990), while others include reports about closeness of interaction between parents and child (Johnson 1986; Wells and Rankin 1988). Most commonly, researchers interested in attachment and delinquency obtain some measure relating to general feelings of closeness to parent(s) (e.g., Aseltine 1995; Glueck and Glueck 1950; Johnson 1986).

The closeness and security of the parent-child bond in infants and very young children is most commonly assessed with the Strange Situation test (see Belsky and Braungart 1991). This test is an experimental method for observing the adaptation of very young children to being briefly separated and then reunited with parents in a laboratory. While many researchers have pointed to the results of the Strange Situation test to argue that extensive nonparental care results in insecure attachments, others have maintained that such evidence is simply a methodological artifact (see Belsky and Braungart 1991).

Regardless of the merits or shortcomings of this method, the NLSY data contain no such information. The only available measure of parent-child attachment for children under 10 years old is a mother-reported assessment of her child's usual behavioral tendencies with respect to five items that make up an insecure attachment scale. Mothers were asked if their 2-to-5 year olds were difficult to soothe or calm, anxious and or worried when left alone, prone to crying when left alone, or tended to need help with most things. This index has a reliability of .52.

To measure attachment in adolescence, I use a one-item question drawn from the child self-administered supplement that asks, "How close do you feel to your mother?" Here, I did not use items that relate to closeness of interaction between mother and child because attachment should be seen as a perceived or felt bond. Close interaction could, but does not necessarily, reflect high degrees of attachment. I regard close parent-child interaction as a measure of parental support as discussed below.

Maternal Support

Although parental support has not received much systematic empirical attention in delinquency research, there is ample evidence pointing to the criminogenic effects of unsupportive family environments (Cullen 1994). According to Cullen (1994), support from parent to child can be divided into two broad categories: expressive and instrumental. Expressive support would include: warmness in parenting, parental affection, family cohesiveness, intimate communication, and confiding. Instrumental support relates to parental helping behaviors that aid a child in reaching some valued goal. Instrumental support may include: parental planning for child's future, helping with schoolwork, attending child's activities or special events, helping children to get jobs, etc.

For very young children, parental support is largely expressive. Researchers using the NLSY data have captured warmness in parenting and parental affection with a warmth and responsiveness scale (e.g., Menaghan et al. 1997). My warmth and responsiveness scale is an adaptation of the measure used by Menaghan et al. (1997). This six-item index is drawn from interviewer observations of the warmth and responsiveness shown by mothers toward children. I use this scale to assess the relationship between early maternal work, maternal support, and delinquency. The reliability of the warmth and responsiveness scale is .79.

To examine maternal support in adolescence, I operationalized support with items that reflect expressive support. To measure expressive support, I use a five-item index drawn from interviewer observations of mother and child interaction in the home. This index is similar to the maternal warmth and responsiveness scale used for pre-school children, but the items are tailored for school-age children. The reliability of this scale is .76.

Maternal Discipline

Because the use of physical punishment appears to be more critical for pre-school children, I measured early maternal discipline with an item that asks mothers to report the number of times they spanked their child during the last week. This NLSY item has been used by previous researchers interested in the maternal characteristics associated with spanking (e.g., Giles-Sims et al. 1995). This measure of discipline captures only negative or harsh discipline. Unfortunately, the NLSY does not include information that reflects upon positive styles of discipline used on pre-school children.

School Attachment

Wiatrowski, Griswold, and Roberts (1981) suggest that school attachment can be best measured by four separate dimensions: School performance, satisfaction with school, educational expectations, and participation in school activities. I measure school attachment with a single item drawn from the CSAS. This question asks children to report their satisfaction with their school. The responses range from 1, meaning very dissatisfied, to 4, meaning very satisfied.

Marital Conflict

Overt marital conflict is frequently measured using parental reports of the amount and intensity of verbal and physical conflict (e.g., Amato, Loomis, and Booth 1995). The NLSY includes information on the frequency of disagreements on various subjects between the mother and her spouse, as reported by mothers. I sum these 7 items to produce a scale with a reliability of .75. Of course, this estimate of marital conflict is relevant only to two-parent families. The relationship between mother's work, marital conflict, and delinquency, however, will be examined only in a sub-group of married mothers.

Control Variables

Behavioral Problems Index (BPI)

As a host of researchers have demonstrated, behavior problems are increasingly stable as children pass through early childhood and into adolescence. As Menaghan et al. (1997) have argued, adolescent behavior problems and family interaction patterns are strongly influenced by child behavior already established in early childhood. In order to test the hypothesis that the effects of current employment and delinquent pathways are independent of past behavior problems, I introduce a behavioral problems index, measured in 1986, into all models. The reliability of this 28-item index is .90.

AFQT

I measure mother's cognitive ability by her score on the Armed Forces Qualification Test (AFQT), which was administered to all respondents in 1980. Like maternal mastery, an AFQT score can be seen as an individual difference which is likely to influence her life chances and those of her children similarly (see Parcel and Menaghan 1994). I control for AFQT to further isolate the independent effects of maternal employment conditions.

Maternal Education

The mother's educational attainment was measured as the highest grade completed by the mother as of 1992. When examining the effects of early maternal employment, I measure education by the highest grade completed as of 1986.

Neighborhood

Serious patterned delinquency is most common in neighborhoods plagued by joblessness, structural deterioration, and crime and drug addiction (see Currie 1998). Socially disorganized urban centers present numerous obstacles to success for parents and their children. While parents are often forced to choose between drawing public assistance or accepting minimum-wage labor to support their families, children are continuously presented with evidence that there is no easy escape from a life of poverty.

Increasingly, researchers are demonstrating the criminogenic influences of certain neighborhood contexts Based on this research, it is likely that such neighborhoods will be characterized by both low-quality employment and high-levels of delinquency. Those who have unstable, low paying jobs may be likely to live in socially disorganized settings which present children with a variety of delinquency risks.

If mothers with low-status, coercive jobs are more likely to have delinquent children, this association may be largely explained by the neighborhood factors associated with those with low quality jobs. Thus, I controlled for neighborhood characteristics to examine the independent effects of mother's work on delinquency. My measure of neighborhood context is a 3-item scale drawn from maternal responses to questions about the quality of the neighborhood in which they live. Mothers were asked to report whether their neighborhood had a "problem" with crime, disorder, and deterioration. The reliability of this scale is .85.

Structural and Family Background Factors

In all models I controlled for race, sex, and age of study children. Age is an interval measure and race and sex are dummy variables. Race is coded 1=Black or Hispanic and 0=White. In separate equations, the Black and Hispanic children will be isolated from one another to examine any differences between these groups and between these groups and the white sub-group. Sex is coded 0=male and 1=female.

I also controlled for family structure. Family structure is a measure of father's presence in the home. An "intact" family is operationalized as a home where the mother is married and presently co-residing with her partner. Thus, biological fathers, stepfathers, and adoptive fathers are all counted equally. Intact Family is coded 0=no marital partner in the home and 1=marital partner present.

Statistical Analysis

The analysis of the data will be conducted through the use of ordinary least squares regression (OLS). OLS will be used to investigate the direct effect of maternal employment on delinquency and the indirect effects of maternal employment through the delinquency pathways.

My theoretical models posit a causal flow from maternal employment characteristics through delinquency pathways to delinquency, with the pathway variables having a direct effect on delinquent outcomes. I argue that the effects of maternal employment are independent of the individual maternal resources that are likely to influence occupational experiences. Following Parcel and Menaghan (1994), I controlled for two such resources in all models: maternal education and maternal cognitive ability (AFQT). I also included a control for neighborhood effects. The neighborhood variable was used only in equations where the effects of current employment are assessed because early neighborhood measures were not available. As I previously stated, it might be argued that certain employment statuses are likely to be highly correlated with neighborhood types. Welfare reliant families, for example, may often reside in high-crime areas. By controlling for neighborhood type, I give support to the independent effects of maternal work.

Additionally, I expected that current maternal employment would influence current delinquency pathways and delinquency, independent of past child behavioral problems. As Menaghan et al. (1997) have argued, family functioning in early adolescence may reflect parental responses to earlier child behavior problems. Accordingly, I controlled for prior behavior problems in all models to investigate whether the hypothesized effects are independent of past child conduct. The inclusion of the BPI measures did not significantly change the relationship between maternal work and child and family outcomes. All tabled results reflect the results of equations without the BPI measure.

The first model examines the direct effects of maternal employment hours and maternal employment conditions on delinquency and the indirect effects of maternal work on delinquency through the delinquency pathway variables. In this model, non-employed, welfare-reliant, and employed mothers are all included. All non-working mothers (including welfare-reliant) are assigned mean values for work hours. Because working conditions were captured via a series of dummy variables reflecting the three working class fractions, non-employed mothers and welfare-reliant mothers were treated as occupational class categories. As a result, I compared non-working mothers to working mothers located in the three class fractions with respect to effects on family life and delinquency.

In the first equation, I examined the direct effect of maternal employment on delinquency. In this equation, the delinquency index was regressed against the employment/non-employment variables while controlling for maternal resources and child characteristics (age, sex, and race). This equation produced estimates of the direct effects of employment on delinquency before the delinquency pathway variables were taken into account.

Next, I assessed my predictions regarding the direct effects of maternal employment on the pathways to delinquency. Thus, the second equation involved regressing the appropriate delinquency pathway variables against the employment/non-employment variables with mother and child control measures. The results of this equation demonstrated the direct effects of employment on delinquency pathways. This step was taken because my theoretical models predicted that maternal employment works primarily through the specified delinquency pathways to influence delinquency.

In the third, and final, equation of model one, I regressed the delinquency index against maternal employment, and the delinquency pathways. This equation produced estimates for the direct effects of all preceding variables on delinquency. Furthermore, by using this strategy, the final equation produced estimates of the direct effect of maternal employment on delinquency, while controlling for the delinquency pathways. If, as hypothesized, maternal employment influenced delinquency indirectly through the delinquency pathways, then any direct effect of maternal employment found in equation one would be reduced or driven into statistical insignificance by introducing the pathway measures in the final equation.

Additional procedures were conducted to study the relationship between maternal employment and delinquency in more detail. As discussed earlier, I will perform sub-group analyses based on marital status, race, and sex of child. Finally, I will investigate the impact of father's work on delinquency outcomes. This model will include controls for maternal resources and maternal employment in an attempt to compare the effects of mother's and father's work.

Correlational Analysis
One potential problem associated with data used in regression analysis is multicolinearity. Multicolinearity exists when there is a high level of intercorrelation between two or more independent variables (Schroeder, Sjoquist, and Stephan 1986). When multicolinearity exists, independent variables tend to have larger standard errors and thus less precision is associated with coefficient estimates (Schroeder, Sjoquist, and Stephan 1986). To assess the degree of multicolinearity between variables, I computed a correlation matrix. The correlation matrix suggests that multicolinearity is not present because no correlation for any two independent measures is greater than .35. Furthermore, tolerance tests did not detect the presence of multicollinearity.

CHAPTER THREE

Does Maternal Work Cause Delinquency?

All models discussed in this chapter use the continuous hours measure, as opposed to using the series of dummy variables. The results for the continuous measure are reported because dummy hours variables did not detect non-linearity in the effects of maternal work on family relations or on delinquency. Furthermore, family income, rather than maternal wages, is used in all models discussed.

Early Maternal Employment and Delinquency

The analysis of the effects of early employment will proceed through three stages. First, I will present the results of an equation that regresses delinquency on early maternal work, maternal resources, and child characteristics. Next, I will analyze the impact of maternal work, with the mother and child control variables, on three hypothesized pathways to delinquency: spanking, insecure child attachment, and maternal warmth and responsiveness. Finally, the results of a model that regresses delinquency on early maternal work, delinquency pathways, and mother and child controls will be discussed.

The Impact of Early Maternal Employment on Delinquency

Table 4 reports the results of a multiple regression equation that examines the impact of early maternal employment status, with mother and child controls, on the 1994 delinquency index.

As displayed in Table 4, child's sex, child's age and family income are significant predictors of delinquency. In this sample, sex and family income are each inversely related to delinquent involvement. Females are less involved than males in delinquency and increasing family income is associated with lesser involvement in delinquent activities. As the data show, none of the early employment variables, including welfare reliance, are significant predictors of delinquency in 1994. Furthermore, the total model explains a relatively small portion, eight percent, of the variation in delinquency.

The Impact of Early Maternal Employment on Early Pathways to Delinquency

Table 5 reports the results of regression models that examine the effects of early maternal employment status on spanking, insecure attachment, and maternal warmth and responsiveness, controlling for maternal resources and child characteristics. The effects on spanking, insecure attachment, and warmth and responsiveness are displayed in panels one, two and three, respectively.

As shown in Table 5, only child's age and family income have statistically significant influence on mother's use of spanking. As displayed, as child's age increases, spanking decreases. Family income is inversely related to spanking; increasing family income is significantly associated with less spanking of one's child. Although the overall model is statistically significant at .05, the variables included in the equation explain just four percent of the variation in spanking.

Table 5 also illustrates the effects of maternal work, maternal resources, and child characteristics on insecure

Table 4. Impact of Early Maternal Employment Status, with Mother and Child Controls, on the 1994 Delinquency Index.

Variable	B	Beta
Child Characteristics		
Age	.31**	.12
Female	-.59**	-.14
Race	.71	.17
Maternal Characteristics		
AFQT	-.01	-.02
Education	-.01	-.03
Intact Marriage	-.03	-.03
Maternal Employment		
Hours 1986	-.01	-.01
Family Income 1986	-.01	.00
Coercive Controls	.52	.10
Technical Controls	-.10	-.02
Bureaucratic Controls	.24	.03
Welfare	-.20	-.04
Family Income 1992	-.13*	-.10
Hours 1992	-.01	-.03
Child Care		
Family Care	-.22	-.05
Non-Family Private	-.16	-.02
Professional Center	-.28	-.06
Constant	-.71	
R-Square	.08	
Adjusted R-Square	.05	

p<.05*; p<.01**

Table 5. Effects of Early Maternal Employment Status on Spanking, Insecure Attachment, and Maternal Warmth and Responsiveness.

Variable	Insecure Attachment		Warmth and Responsiveness		Spanking	
	B	Beta	B	Beta	B	Beta
Child Characteristics						
Age	-.43*	-.07	-.35**	-.17	-.39*	-.09
Female	.42	.05	.17	.06	-.11	-.02
Race	.67	.08	-.15	-.05	-.36	-.05
Maternal Characteristics						
AFQT	-.87'	-.22	.16**	.12	-.24	-.08
Education	-.02	-.01	.01	.03	.01	.01
Intact Marriage	-.56	-.06	-.00	-.02	.01	.00
Maternal Employment						
Hours 1986	.01	.04	.01	.02	-.01	-.02
Family Income 1986	.07	.02	-.01	-.01	-.09	.04
Coercive Controls	-.12	-.01	.17	.04	.25	.03
Technical Controls	.20	.02	.08	.02	.20	.02
Bureaucratic Controls	-.02	-.02	-.04	-.01	.70	.06
Welfare	-.08	-.01	-.04	-.01	.03	.01
Family Income 1992	-.16	-.06	.05	.06	-.23*	-.11
Hours 1992	-.01	-.02	-.00	-.00	-.01	-.04
Child Care						
Family Care	.30	.03	.01	.01	-.53	-.07
Non-Family Private	-.45	-.03	.18	.03	.32	.02
Professional Center	.52	.05	-.00	-.00	-.43	-.06
Constant	25.84		8.10		9.90	
R-Square	.08'		.10**		.04*	
Adjusted R-Square	.06		.08		.02	

p<.05 p<.01**

child attachment. Child's age and maternal AFQT are shown to be influential on insecure child attachment. According to the data, the signs of insecure attachment diminish as children get older. Moreover, the offspring of mothers with higher AFQT scores show decreasing symptoms of insecure attachment.

The variables that measure employment status and workplace experiences are not significantly associated with insecure attachment. The combination of resource, child, and employment variables explains eight percent of the variation in insecure attachment and the model is significant at .001.

Finally, Table 5 reports the effects of early maternal employment, maternal resources, and child characteristics on maternal warmth and responsiveness. Here, the data show that child's age and maternal AFQT have significant effects on the amount of warmth and responsiveness directed from mother to child. According to the data, being older is associated with lesser maternal warmth and responsiveness. Furthermore, as maternal AFQT increases, so too does the amount of warmth and responsiveness bestowed on children.

The overall model is significant at .001 and the variables included explain ten percent of the variation in maternal warmth and responsiveness.

Early Maternal Employment, Early Pathways, and Delinquency

Table 6 reports the effects of maternal resources, child characteristics, and delinquency pathways on delinquency. As the table illustrates, child's sex, child's age and family income remain significantly associated with delinquency. Introducing the pathways variables--spanking, warmth and responsiveness, and insecure attachment--does not diminish the influence of these variables. This finding suggests that the sex and age of the child and family income are related to delinquency through processes not measured by the three early pathway variables used in the analysis.

Furthermore, none of the early pathway variables exhibited a significant influence on delinquent involvement. And the addition of spanking, warmth and responsiveness, and insecure attachment did not contribute any additional explained variation over the model that consisted only of maternal resources, child characteristics, and maternal employment. In this particular sample, spanking, maternal warmth and responsiveness, and insecure attachment cannot be considered "pathways" to delinquency.

The Impact of Current Maternal Employment on Delinquency

The analysis of the current employment model proceeded through three stages. First, I present a table depicting the effects of current maternal work controlling for maternal resources and child characteristics, on delinquency. Next I analyzed the influence of maternal work, with the appropriate control variables, on five delinquency pathway variables: delinquent peers, school attachment, warmth and responsiveness, child attachment, and maternal supervision.

Finally, the results of an equation which regresses delinquency on maternal work, delinquency pathways, and control variables were analyzed.

Current Maternal Employment and Delinquency

As shown in Table 7, child's age, child's sex, and family income are significant predictors of delinquent involvement. According to the data, being older and being male are associated with greater involvement in

Table 6. Effects of Early Maternal Employment, Child Characteristics, and Delinquency Pathways on Delinquency.

Variable	B	Beta
Child Characteristics		
Age	.31**	.11
Female	-.58**	-.14
Race	.72	.17
Maternal Characteristics		
AFQT	-.07	-.04
Education	-.01	-.03
Intact Marriage	-.04	-.01
Maternal Employment		
Hours 1986	-.00	-.01
Family Income 1986	.01	.00
Coercive Controls	.52	.10
Technical Controls	-.09	-.02
Bureaucratic Controls	.23	.03
Welfare	-.20	-.04
Family Income 1992	-.13*	-.10
Hours 1992	-.01	-.03
Child Care		
Family Care	-.22	-.04
Non-Family Private	-.16	-.02
Professional Center	-.27	-.06
Delinquency Pathways		
Insecure Attachment	-.01	-.02
Warmth and Responsiveness	-.02	-.02
Spanking	.01	.02
Constant	-.41	
R-Square	.08**	
Adjusted R-Square	.05	

p<.05 p<.01**

delinquency. Moreover, as family income increases, involvement in delinquency falls. Consistent with the early employment model, none of the current employment categories exert influence on delinquency. The overall model is significant at .001 and these variables combine to explain seven percent of the variation in delinquency.

Current Maternal Employment and the Pathways to
Delinquency

Table 8 consists of five panels representing the effects of current maternal work on five variables used to measure delinquency risks.

Table 8 depicts the effects of current work and control variables on delinquent peer association. As displayed, child's sex and neighborhood disorder were found to be significant influences on the degree to which children experience pressure from peers to behave in a delinquent manner. The figures indicate that males experience significantly more pressure to engage in delinquency. Furthermore, children living in socially disorganized communities were relatively more involved with delinquent peers. This model is significant at .001 and the variables included explain four percent of the variation in delinquent peer association.

Maternal supervision is significantly influenced by child's age and sex, hours of paid employment, and by workplace controls. First, female children are more closely supervised than their male counterparts. Next, paid employment appears to have a complex influence on maternal supervision. Employment hours are positively, but very weakly, related to supervision. This suggests that greater maternal involvement in the paid workforce results in a higher level of maternal supervision of children. Working, then, enhances a mother's active supervision of her child's activities. On the other hand, being employed in a bureaucratically-controlled setting reduces maternal supervision. Compared to non-employed mothers, female professionals (bureaucratic settings) are less involved in the supervision of their children. The overall model achieved significance at .01 and this group of variables explained five percent of the total variation in supervision.

Table 7. The Impact of Current Maternal Employment, with Mother and Child Controls, on Delinquency.

Variable	B	Beta
Child Characteristics		
Age	.30**	.11
Female	-.59**	-.14
Race	.69	.16
Maternal Characteristics		
AFQT	-.01	-.01
Education	-.06	-.07
Intact Marriage	-.07	-.02
Maternal Employment		
Hours 1992	-.01	-.04
Family Income 1992	-.09*	.07
Coercive Controls	-.07	-.02
Technical Controls	-.03	-.01
Bureaucratic Controls	.16	.03
Welfare	.19	.03
Neighborhood Disorder	-.03	-.03
Constant	-1.17	
R-Square	.07**	
Adjusted R-Square	.05	

p < .05*; p < .01**

Table 8. 1994 Delinquency Pathways: The Impact of 1992 Maternal Employment.

Variable	Supervision		Delinquent Peers		Warmth and Responsiveness		Attachment		School Attachment	
	B	Beta	B	Beta	B	Beta	B	Beta	B	Beta
Child Characteristics										
Age	-.14**	-.11	.01	.03	-.02	-.04	-.10	-.05	-.01	-.01
Female	.20**	.10	-.23**	-.12	-.14*	.07	.22*	.08	.18*	.10
Race	-.31	-.17	.00	.01	.01	.04	.32	.02	.11	-.06
Mat. Characteristics										
AFQT	-.00	-.01	-.00	-.01	.01*	.09	.16*	.13	-.00	-.00
Education	.01	.02	-.05	.01	.01	.02	-.01	-.01	.01	.01
Intact Marriage	-.11	-.06	-.01	-.01	.13	.07	.01	.00	-.01	-.00
Mat. Employment										
Hours 1992	.01*	.08*	-.01	-.04	.00	.01	.00	.00	.00	.00
Family Income 1992	.03	.06	.00	.03	.06*	.08	.01	.01	.04*	.09
Coercive Controls	-.01	-.03	-.01	-.04	-.00	-.00	-.03	-.01	-.01	-.04
Technical Controls	-.13	-.06	-.01	-.04	.00	.00	-.13	-.04	.07	.03
Bureaucratic Controls	-.32*	-.12	.01	.02	.01	.02	-.06	-.02	-.01	-.02
Welfare	-.01	-.04	.01	.03	-.19*	-.07	.14	.04	.08	.04
Neighborhood Disorder	-.01	-	.04*	.08	-.01	-.01	-.04	-.07	.02	.07
Constant	4.65		.60		3.74		7.33		2.70	
R-Square	.05*		.04*		.06*		.03		.03	
Adjusted R-Square	.03		.02		.04		.01		.01	

*p<.05; **p<.01

Maternal warmth and responsiveness, is significantly related to child's age, maternal AFQT, family income, and welfare reliance. Here, higher maternal AFQT scores are associated with greater maternal warmth. Furthermore, an increase in total family income brings a significant increase in maternal warmth. Finally, current welfare reliance is inversely related to maternal warmth. Compared to non-working mothers who are not on welfare, mothers who rely on welfare are less warm and responsive in their parenting.

The study child's attachment to school is significantly influenced by child's sex and family income. The data show that females feel a stronger attachment to school than do males. This model is significant at .05 and the combined variables explain just three percent of the total variation in school attachment.

The effects of maternal work and control variables on mother-child attachment are displayed. Both child's sex and AFQT exert significant influence on mother-child attachment. Girls and children with mothers with relatively higher AFQT ability are more attached to mothers. This combination of measures explains just three percent of the total variation in mother-child attachment.

As illustrated in Table 8, current maternal employment exerts little influence on the pathway variables. The number of hours spent in paid employment, for example, is predictive only of maternal supervision. Furthermore, the positive effect of work hours on supervision is very modest in size. Family income is positively related to maternal warmth and responsiveness, and to school attachment. The occupational class variables are shown to have almost no effect at all on the delinquency pathway variables. The one significant finding is the small, inverse effect of having a bureaucratically-controlled job on maternal supervision. Finally, welfare reliance is shown to be inversely related to warmth and responsiveness.

*The Impact of Current Maternal Employment and
Delinquency Pathways on Delinquency*

Table 9 reports the influence of mother's current employment status, delinquency pathways, and control variables on delinquency.

As the table suggests, several of the delinquency pathways exert direct influence on delinquency. The negative effect of family income on delinquency, however, is rendered non-significant after controlling for the delinquency pathways.

Table 9 shows that greater maternal supervision, greater school attachment, and lesser delinquent peer influence are all associated with less delinquent involvement. That is, controlling for maternal resources, child characteristics, and mother's work, those children who like school, are supervised more strictly, and who have relatively fewer delinquent peer associations, are less involved in delinquent activities.

The Effects of Early Maternal Employment on Delinquency in the Married and Single Mother Sub-Groups

An analysis of the effects of maternal employment within single mother and married mother sub-groups was performed. No significant differences with respect to the effects of the variables were found between the two sub-groups. Neither the early employment variables nor the early delinquency pathway measures were significantly

Table 9. 1994 Delinquency: The Impact of 1992 Maternal Employment and Current Pathways on Delinquency.

Variable	B	Beta
Child Characteristics		
Age	.26**	.09
Female	-.48**	-.12
Race	.74	.18
Maternal Characteristics		
AFQT	-.01	-.01
Education	-.06	-.07
Intact Marriage	-.08	-.02
Maternal Employment		
Hours 1992	-.00	-.02
Family Income 1992	-.01	-.05
Coercive Controls	-.03	-.01
Technical Controls	.01	.00
Bureaucratic Controls	.06	.01
Welfare	.22	.04
Delinquency Pathways		
Supervision	-.28**	-.12
Delinquent Peer Association	.27**	.13
Warmth and Responsiveness	-.04	-.02
Attachment	-.05	-.04
School Attachment	-.87**	-.11
Neighborhood Disorder	.01	.02
Constant	2.30	
R-Square	.13**	
Adjusted R-Square	.11	

p < .05*; p < .01**

predictive of delinquency for either the married mother or single mother sub-group. Furthermore, early marital conflict is not significantly influenced by maternal employment status nor does it have a significant impact on delinquency in 1994.

The Effects of Current Maternal Employment on Delinquency in the Married and Single Mother Sub-Groups

The sub-group analysis was based on maternal marital status for the current employment sample. Few differences were found between the married and single mother groups.
Single Mothers 1992. For single mothers, no employment status variable was either directly or indirectly influential on delinquency. Some aspects of maternal employment, however, were predictive of several of the delinquency pathway variables. Consistent with several of the models discussed in this analysis, welfare reliance is inversely related to maternal warmth and responsiveness for the single mother group. Further, among single mothers, mother-child attachment was significantly associated with one employment status variable -- technical control. Compared to non-working mothers, then, single mothers who work under technical controls were, on average, more warm and responsive toward their children.

One employment measure had a significant effect on maternal supervision. Compared to non-working single mothers, single mothers who worked under bureaucratic controls exerted less supervision over their children.

Although current employment status is related to several of the delinquency pathway measures for single mothers, none of these pathway variables was significantly predictive of delinquency. Therefore, maternal employment was not even indirectly related to delinquency in the single-mother group.

Married Mothers 1992. As with the single mother group, welfare reliance was inversely related to warmth and responsiveness in the married-mother group. This finding was consistent throughout the analysis and implied that severe economic disadvantage places strains on mothers that are observable in the way they treat their children.

One employment variable exerted significant influence on child's school attachment. Compared to the children of non-working mothers, the children of mothers who work under bureaucratic controls were *less* attached to school. Furthermore, school attachment was inversely related to delinquency in the married-mother sample.

Therefore, although the effect was indirect and not strong, being the child of a professionally-employed mother was associated with less school attachment and, thus, greater delinquent involvement. Marital conflict in 1992 was neither influenced by maternal employment, nor was it a significant predictor of delinquency.

The Impact of Early Maternal Employment on Delinquency in the White and Non-White Sub-Groups

Significant differences were found between the White and Non-White sub-groups. Table 10 displays the effects of early employment, with mother and child controls, on delinquency. Panel one shows the effects for Whites, while panel two contains the effects for Non-Whites.

The data found in panel one of Table 10 show that, for White mothers and children, child's sex and early employment experiences exerted significant influence on delinquency in 1994. The significant effect for coercive controls found in panel one suggests that compared to the children of non-working White mothers, the children of White mothers who work under coercive controls had greater delinquent involvement in 1994. While early coercive work controls have a positive influence on delinquency in 1994 for the White sub-sample, no such effect was found in the Non-White group. Under panel two (Non-Whites), the only significant predictor of delinquency was child's sex. Here, as throughout the analysis, females had less delinquent involvement than males. This sub-group analysis by race, then, implies that variation in early maternal work experiences are a more important factor for the White children in this sample than for the Black and Hispanic children included in the Non-White category.

Both the White model and the Non-White model are significant at the .05 probability level. The combined variables for the White and Non-White sub-groups, explain ten percent and eight percent, respectively, of the variation in delinquency.

The Effects of Early Maternal Employment on Delinquency Pathways in the White and Non-White Sub-Groups

In order to bring understanding to the racial group differences found in Table 10, the early delinquency pathways were regressed on the employment variables for both race sub-groups. The differences may be due to differences in parenting practices between the two groups.

Table 11 displays the effects of early employment on the delinquency pathways for Whites and Non-Whites. Panels one through three illustrate the effects for the White sub-group and panels four through six show the significant associations for the Non-White group. As Table 11 indicates, there are few substantial differences between the White and Non-White groups with respect to spanking, insecure attachment, and warmth and responsiveness. Most notably, the effects of coercive work controls do not differ substantially by racial group. This finding is noteworthy because racial differences in early parenting practices may have helped to explain the different early employment status effects on delinquency. Working under coercive

Table 10. 1994 Delinquency: The Impact of 1986 Maternal Employment for Whites (N = 255) and Non-Whites (N = 452).

Variables	Whites 1		Non-Whites 2	
	B	Beta	B	Beta
Child Characteristics				
Age	.01	.03	.01	.06
Female	-.62***	-.17	-.60***	-.15
Maternal Characteristics				
Maternal AFQT	-.00	-.01	-.01	-.07
Maternal Education	-.08	-.08	-.08	-.10
Intact Marriage	-.33	-.08	-.05	-.01
Maternal Employment				
Hours 1986	.00	.01	.00	.01
Family Income	.15	.10	.06	.04
Coercive Control	.62**	.15	-.16	-.03
Technical Control	-.20	-.03	.27	.03
Bureaucratic Control	-.20	-.03	-.21	-.05
Welfare	.70	.11	-.21	-.05
Constant	3.3		4.2	
R-Squared	.10***		.07***	
Adjusted R-Squared	.06		.04	

**p < .05, *** p < .01

conditions, however, do not appear to have divergent effects that depend upon race.

The Effects of Early Maternal Employment and Delinquency Pathways on Delinquency in the White and Non-White Sub-Groups

Table 12 displays the effects of early maternal work and early delinquency pathways on delinquency in 1994. The effects for Whites and Non-Whites are under panel one and panel two, respectively. As depicted in the table, the children of White mothers who worked under coercive controls in 1986 are more involved in delinquent activities in 1994, even after controlling for the delinquency pathway measures. This result is not surprising given that coercive work controls were not predictive of any of the delinquency pathways. This finding implies that, for Whites, the effect of early coercive work on later delinquency operates through mechanisms not captured by the early pathways.

Finally, early delinquency pathways do not exert significant influence on delinquency for either the White or Non- White subgroups. Furthermore, the addition of the early pathway variables add no additional explained variation of the delinquency index over the model that included only maternal work and controls.

The Effects of Current Maternal Employment within the White and Non-White Sub-Groups

One major difference in the effects of current employment was discovered between the White and Non-White sub-groups (tables not included). This difference is found in the impact of current family income on delinquency. In the first equation, where delinquency is regressed on current

Table 11. 1986 Delinquency Pathways: The Impact of 1986 Maternal Employment for Whites (N = 452) and Non-Whites (N = 25).

Variable	Spanking 1		Whites Insecure Attachment 2		Warmth and Responsiveness 3		Spanking 4		Non-Whites Insecure Attachment 5		Warmth and Responsiveness 6	
	B	Beta	B	Beta	B	Beta	B	Beta	B	Bet	B	Beta
Child												
Age	-.04**	-.13	-.04	-.08	-.006	-.05	-.04	-.09	-.04	-.08	-.005	-.001
Female	.16	.03	-.08	-.01	-.10	-.05	-.38	-.05	.89**	.09	.16	.06
Maternal Characteristics												
Maternal AFQT	-.02**	-.16	-.04***	-.24	.001	.04	-.02**	-.11	-.02	-.09	.01***	.18
Maternal Education	-.07	-.05	-.16	-.07	.004	.008	.16	.09	-.06	-.03	-.003	-.005
Intact Marriage	.76	.13	-.48	-.05	-.07	-.03	.08	.01	-.10	-.12	-.10	-.04
Maternal Employment												
Hours 1986	-.01	-.05	.02	.05	-.005	-.05	-.01	-.02	-.01	-.02	.01	.07
Family Income	-.33**	-.17	.06	.02	.009	.01	-.10	-.03	-.03	-.01	-.03	-.03
Coercive Control	-.35	-.06	-.33	-.04	-.07	-.03	.40	.04	-.29	-.02	.04	.01
Technical Control	-.32	-.05	-.58	-.06	-.09	.03	.12	.01	.78	.06	.30	.09
Bureaucratic Control	.46	.05	.82	.05	-.11	.03	.37	.02	.43	.02	-.29	-.06
Welfare	-.56	-.06	-.31	-.02	-.23	.06	.52	.06	.15	.02	-.24	-.09
Constant	6.2		24.3		3.7		3.9		23.6		1.7	
R-Squared	.08***		.09***		.02		.03		.05***		.08***	
Adjusted R-Square	.05		.06		.00		.004		.03		.05	

**p < .05; p < .01.

Table 12. 1994 Delinquency: The Impact of Early Maternal Employment and Delinquency Pathways for Whites (N = 255) and Non-Whites (N = 452).

Variable	Whites 1		Non-Whites 2	
	B	**Beta**	**B**	**Beta**
Child Characteristics				
Age	.004	.02	.01	.05
Female	-.61***	-.16	-.55***	-.13
Maternal Characteristics				
Maternal AFQT	-.002	-.03	-.007	-.07
Maternal Education	-.09	-.09	-.09	-.09
Intact Marriage	-.28	-.07	-.10	-.03
Maternal Employment				
Hours 1986	.004	.01	-.003	-.01
Family Income	.15	.10	.05	.03
Coercive Control	.61**	.14	-.20	-.04
Technical Control	-.02	-.15	-.30	-.06
Bureaucratic Control	-.13	-.02	.21	.03
Welfare	.70	.11	-.21	-.05
Delinquency Pathways				
Spanking	-.04	-.05	.02	.05
Insecure Attachment	-.02	-.04	-.02	-.05
Warmth and Responsiveness	.10	.06	-.08	-.05
Constant	3.75		5.14	
R-Squared	.11***		.07***	
Adjusted R-Squared	.06		.04	

**p < .05. ***p < .01
Note: reference category for employment dummies is non-worker mothers not receiving welfare.

mother's work and mother and child controls, higher family income is associated with less delinquency for the Non-White group but not for the White group. This finding suggests that, in this particular sample, family economic resources are a more powerful protective factor for young minorities than for young Whites.

To further investigate the process through which income affects delinquency, racial differences in the effects of current family income on the delinquency pathways were assessed. Few racial differences in the effects of family income were found. In fact, for the Non-White group, family income is not a significant influence on any of the pathways to delinquency. For the White sub-group, higher income is associated with greater maternal warmth and higher school attachment. This finding suggests that the benefits minority youths reap from economic resources operate through processes not captured by the delinquency pathway measures.

Finally, by introducing the delinquency pathways in the final equation, the negative effect of family income on delinquency is rendered non-significant for Non-Whites. Family income for Non-Whites, then, may operate partially through the pathway variables to influence delinquency, though these effects were not detected in the analysis detailed above.

The Impact of Early Maternal Employment in the Male and Female Sub-Groups

The sub-group analysis by child's sex did not shed additional insight into the relationship between early maternal employment and delinquency. Neither the early maternal work variables nor early pathway measures were significant predictive of delinquency for female or male children.

The Effect of Current Maternal Employment in the Male and Female Sub-Groups

The effects of current maternal employment do not appear to differ markedly between boys and girls. The few contrasts between males and females are detailed below (tables not included).

In the first equation, boys and girls are contrasted with respect to the impact of maternal work and mother and child controls on delinquency. This model produced one notable finding. For females, family income serves to decrease delinquent involvement while, for boys, increasing maternal education reduces delinquency.

As for the effects of mother's current work on the delinquency pathways, only one major difference based on sex was revealed. Here, the daughters of mothers who work under bureaucratic controls are supervised to a lesser degree. This relationship does not, however, exist in the male sub-group. Professional mothers, it appears, are less active in supervising their daughters, but no less involved in supervising their sons.

Finally, the negative effect of family income on delinquency in girls remains intact even after the delinquency pathways are introduced into the final model. Similarly, greater maternal education remains as a negative influence on delinquency in boys when the delinquency pathways are included.

The Influence of Father's Employment on Delinquency

The impact of father's early and current employment status and hours worked on delinquency was examined. With professional fathers (i.e., those experiencing bureaucratic controls) as the reference category, the effects of father's work were assessed. Controls for mother and child characteristics, family income, and maternal employment hours were also included in this model.

No significant effects on delinquency for either the early or current father's employment model were detected. Father's early employment did, however, exert influence on early maternal warmth and responsiveness. Compared to women married to professionals (fraction three), those mothers married to fraction one or fraction two workers are less warm and responsive toward children. This finding implies that the conditions of paternal employment exert influence on family processes that are observable in the manner in which mothers treat their children. In this case, when fathers work in positions where autonomy and self-direction are less common, mothers appear to be less nurturing and supportive in interaction with children. Early maternal warmth and responsiveness is not predictive of later delinquency. Thus, father's work does not work indirectly through mother's parenting style to influence delinquency.

CHAPTER 4

Conclusion

Are the children of working mothers more likely to be delinquent than other children? According to the few past studies focused on this issue, and according to the results of this analysis, the answer is a qualified "No." There are no strong findings anywhere in the literature suggesting that maternal work is criminogenic. Although a positive relationship between maternal employment and delinquency was found in a few of the early investigations (e.g., Glueck and Glueck 1950; Hirschi 1969; Nye 1963), more recent work implies that there is no effect at all or that having a working mother is sometimes associated with less delinquency (e.g., Broidy 1995; Farnworth 1984; Zhao et al. 1997).

In fact, even if maternal employment is, in some cases, weakly related to delinquency, no researcher has ever identified maternal employment as an important predictor of delinquent behavior. With respect to delinquency, it seems, it does not matter very much whether or not or how much mothers work. So, why have so many social commentators, politicians, and average citizens shown concern that maternal employment might contribute to our relatively high crime rate?

The debate over the behavioral effects of maternal employment continues on today in newspaper editorials with titles such as "Why Mothers Should Stay Home," in Dr. Laura Schlessinger's popular radio show, and in prime time news programs (Chira 1998). Rarely do these media portrayals of the negative consequences of maternal work cite the large body of research findings suggesting that the children of working mothers are generally no worse off than other children. Maternal employment, as a perceived social problem, has a long history in America.

According to Chira (1998), the scapegoating of working women can be traced back to the Great Depression when women were depicted in the popular media and government publications as stealing jobs from men. Even as women, if only briefly, were encouraged to work to support the World War II effort, television shows and Hollywood films celebrated the sacrificial housewife and portrayed negatively those women who dared to search for fulfillment in paid careers. Meanwhile, the post-World War II Congress held hearings about the risks associated with maternal employment and Freudian psychologists added authoritative warnings to the debate. These widespread concerns, however, were largely born out of cultural ideals and the apprehensions created by a rapidly changing society. Scientific research rarely supported the fervor against the working mother.

Rather than being a social problem whose untoward effects can be demonstrated by empirical data, then, the maternal employment-delinquency connection is better described as a socially constructed problem.

As the construction of social problems go, the identification of maternal employment as a societal risk follows a fairly simple argument: a child is "at risk" when a mother works because he or she misses out on the nurturing, teaching, and discipline that a "stay-at home" mother can provide. The love and guidance of a mother is seen as critical to the development of a child, and most alternatives to a mother (e.g., babysitters, childcare providers) are seen as poor substitutes.

There is little doubt that early relations between parents and children are extremely important to the development of children and to their psychological adjustment and achievements throughout life. The formation of a secure attachment to one's mother, for example, is a strong predictor of later outcomes (Liebert and Wicks-Nelson 1981). And many variables associated with parenting (e.g., neglect, disciplinary style) are consistent predictors of delinquency (see Benson 2002).

Fueled by these facts and by cherished popular beliefs in the sanctity of the "first relationship"--the coupling of mother and child-- for decades politicians and social commentators have pointed to modern trends in work and family life to explain social problems such as crime. What some critics of maternal employment have implied is that if society is more disordered, more criminal, and more violent than it once was, maybe it has something to do with the production of several generations of mother-deprived children. If the unprecedented entrance of mothers in the workforce is somehow related to crime, then, it must be because working mothers fail their children by depriving them of the support and discipline they need.

Following this logic, parenting should mediate the relationship between work and delinquency activity. If maternal employment causes delinquency, it must be because working mothers parent their children less often or less effectively. Maternal work might promote delinquency because it influences important delinquency risks factors associated with family life (e.g., supervision, support, and discipline). As the results of the current study show, however, the characteristics of maternal work have relatively little or no effect on delinquency either directly or indirectly through the largely family-oriented delinquency pathways. The present study has shown that regardless of how this issue was examined, having a working mother has only small effects and those effects are not consistently criminogenic. This general pattern cuts across almost all samples and sub-samples identified: early versus later work; married versus non-married; Non-Whites versus Whites.

In the remaining pages, I will reiterate my findings, highlighting the few significant effects of mother's work that were found. Next, I will note the limitations of the current study, suggest direction for future research, and discuss the policy implications of this study.

Interpreting the Effects of Early Maternal Work on Delinquency

The results of my analysis are consistent with the large body of work that has reported little or no influence of early maternal employment on child outcomes (see Harvey 1999; Scarr et al. 1987). In this section, I will return to the substantive findings of the analysis and will attempt to interpret the meanings of those effects and non-effects that were revealed.

In the full sample consisting of all employed mothers, welfare-reliant mothers, and non-working mothers, only one significant effect related to employment status was found. This effect relates to the influence of employment status on maternal warmth and responsiveness. Compared to non-working mothers not receiving welfare, welfare-reliant mothers were found to be less warm and responsive with children. This result is consistent with past work that has informed us that the economic deprivation accompanying welfare dependence places severe strains on parents which shapes their interactions with offspring.

The fact that welfare reliance negatively influences parenting, even when controlling for maternal resources (AFQT, maternal education), suggests that economic disadvantage is one external stressor on family life, and that this effect is independent of a mother's intrapersonal resources. It may be that severe economic disadvantage presents a mother with a constellation of strains which, consciously felt or not in the form of stress, result in less patience and warmth with children.

In the full sample, beyond the association between employment status and maternal warmth, no early employment variables were predictive of either the early delinquency pathways or of delinquency. Thus, virtually all of the theories predicting that lower quality work in the early years would negatively affect family life and later delinquency were not confirmed.

Given past research on the effects of maternal employment, it is not surprising that mother's early work had little or no effect on the delinquency pathways or on delinquency. I did not expect mother's early employment to influence delinquency directly; instead, I predicted that early work would have an indirect impact on delinquent activity through the three early delinquent pathways: insecure attachment, maternal warmth and responsiveness, and spanking.

As discussed previously, none of the early employment variables was predictive of a child's degree of insecure attachment. This finding is consistent with most past findings. While some researchers have reported lower levels of mother-attachment among pre-schoolers raised in nonparental care (e.g., Belsky 1988, Schwartz 1983), the most recent set of findings suggest otherwise. As Chira (1998) has reported, most researchers have concluded that early day-care experiences pose little threat to the mother-child bond.

I did expect that high quality working conditions, higher wages or income, and greater work supports would be associated with higher mother-child attachment. These predictions were based on theory and research that suggests that the quality of family relations should be positively affected by better working conditions (Colvin and Pauly 1983; Rogers et al. 1991). This was not supported by the data.

Like insecure attachment, mother's use of spanking was not statistically linked to any of the measures of maternal work. This result, again, was not surprising since hours spent in paid employment has not been identified as a predictor of maternal spanking (Giles-Sims et al. 1996).

While I did not expect work, in and of itself, to influence the use of spanking, I did predict that higher quality employment would be linked to less spanking. This prediction was based on research that has detected a higher rate of the use of physical punishment among low-income populations (Gelles 1978). These past findings may, in part, be explained by the unrewarding and stressful jobs held by those in the low-income population. Such jobs may place strains on parents, which could reduce parenting skills. Consistent with this perspective, I did find that increasing family income reduces maternal spanking. This may reflect the way that economic stressors shape parenting styles. Economic strain may produce coercive parenting.

The most surprising set of findings for the effects of early work and parenting on later delinquency was the failure to identify significant effects of early maternal warmth and responsiveness, spanking, or insecure attachment on later delinquency. Warm and responsive parenting has been consistently linked with various kinds of positive outcomes for children (Rollins and Thomas 1979). And Loeber and Stouthamer-Loeber (1986) reported evidence that early positive and nurturing parenting styles pay dividends later on in terms of less delinquency and behavioral problems in children.

A link between early parenting style and later delinquency may not have been detected here for several reasons. First, the style of parenting detected in a child's pre-school years may or may not be predictive of parenting throughout childhood and adolescence. Most of the children in this sample were first or second born children to relatively young mothers. One possibility is that the quality of parent-child relations improved as mothers aged. Poor quality parenting among younger mothers may be a reflection of low emotional maturity and may, in fact, improve as mothers age.

Second, the measurement of warm and responsive parenting may be influenced due to observational effects: this measure of parenting was obtained by interviewers who observed mothers and children in the home and recorded their observations. A better measure of supportive parenting might be obtained through less obtrusive techniques, such as surveying children about the amount of love, nurturing, and support that they receive from parents.

Finally, early insecure attachment had no observable influence on later delinquency. This finding is not consistent with those past results identifying mother-child attachment as a solid predictor of delinquency. Like parenting style, however, mother-child attachment may change over time so that insecurely attached pre-schoolers may well have stronger bonds with their mothers in adolescence. Early attachment may be an important influence on child outcomes, but as Sampson and Laub have argued (1993, 1994) the quality and intensity of social bonds may vary throughout the life course depending upon structural influences, life changes, and the impact of other risk factors.

Interpreting the Race Effect of Early Coercive Work on Delinquency

Although the quality of mother's early work did not influence delinquency in the full sample, some effects of workplace controls were identified in the White sub-sample. Consistent with my predictions for the general effects of early maternal working conditions on later delinquency, I found that the children of White mothers who worked under coercive controls in the child's pre-school years had greater delinquent involvement in adolescence.

This finding supports the theoretical contentions of Colvin and Pauly (1983), who argued that coercive parental work places strains on family relations which predispose children to misbehavior in school, association with delinquent peers and, ultimately, delinquent activity. While the White sub-group analysis did identify a criminogenic effect of having a mother employed in a coercive setting, this effect was not accounted for by considering the mediating effects of family relations. Contrary to the theoretical statement of Colvin and Pauly (1983), the criminogenic influence of coercive maternal work remained after controlling for the early delinquency pathways. This result suggests that the detrimental impact of coercive maternal work affects children in ways not accounted for by the early delinquency pathways.

One unexpected finding was the absence of effects for early coercive work for Non-White mothers on later delinquency. In other words, why is it that White children displayed more delinquency when their mothers had coercive jobs, but Non-White children did not? This finding may be interpreted in a variety of ways. First, non-white women are dramatically overrepresented in the secondary labor market. Due to lower levels of human capital, structural disadvantage, and institutional discrimination, Non-Whites make up a substantial portion of the secondary labor market workforce (Edwards 1979). Therefore, it is likely that Non-White mothers working in coercive settings are more accustomed than whites to such work environments and, thus, are more tolerant of the conditions.

Second, Non-White workers in fraction one jobs may be more likely to find peer support in such settings since they are likely to work alongside many others who share their racial and socioeconomic status. Whites, on the other hand, may often find themselves to be part of the minority when working in fraction one jobs. The strains of this type of work may take a greater toll on White workers, then, if they experience a lesser degree of co-worker support than their Non-White counterparts. Because social support is a critical part of the adjustment to difficult work experiences (House 1982), this explanation may help to explain the differential race effects of work.

Finally, Non-White families may not show a negative effect of coercive work because the alternative to any kind of work, including low-paying, non-advancing work, may often be welfare dependence or poverty (Baca-Zinn 1987; Farnworth 1984; Vandell and Ramanen 1992). Researchers, for example, have demonstrated that low-income, African-American children tend to score higher on achievement tests when their mothers are employed (e.g., Milne et al. 1986). Due to the constellation of disadvantages met by many Black and Hispanic families, being employed, even in a secondary market job, may serve as a buffer against harsh economic conditions.

Interpreting the Effects of Current Maternal Employment on Delinquency

In Chapter One, the various theoretical perspectives discussed suggested certain effects of current maternal employment and current delinquency pathways on delinquency. As with the predicted effects of early employment, few of the current employment hypotheses were supported by the data. A few significant effects were detected. These associations, however, were not strong and were not consistently criminogenic.

One noteworthy finding was the inverse relationship between current family income and delinquency. As discussed previously, in the full sample, increases in current family income resulted in decreases in delinquency, even when controlling for the delinquent pathway variables. This is a significant finding because criminologists have debated the impact of socioeconomic status on delinquency for decades, and the most recent and comprehensive statement on the matter is that, in the majority of studies, social class does not contribute greatly to delinquent involvement (Tittle and Meier 1990).

Tittle and Meier (1990:1983) argue that the "relationship between social class and criminal behavior is one of the most important and perennial issues in the sociology of crime". Over the last fifty years, researchers have used a wide variety of samples, methodologies, and analytic strategies to tease out the "true" effects of class on delinquency. Despite these efforts, criminologists have reached no clear consensus on identifying the nature of the SES/delinquency relationship.

Our lack of understanding about the class-delinquency relationship is troublesome given that many criminological theories place a great deal of emphasis on the importance of economic resources and opportunities in contributing to involvement in criminal behavior. Furthermore, ever since the 1960s, legislation pointed at reducing poverty and creating a larger menu of opportunity for underclass youths was expected to lower national crime rates.

When national crime did not decrease following the anti-poverty programs of the sixties, criminologists argued over the implications. Many critics of the "Great Society" programs pointed to rising crime rates as yet another failure of shortsighted liberal policies (Murray 1982; Wilson 1983). These programs, it has been argued, merely served to increase inequality in America by producing a larger underclass through welfare dependence and by failing to create lasting jobs with livable ways and room for upward mobility (Currie 1985).

The debate over the impact of opportunity expanding jobs programs, then, lends continuing importance to the study of the relationship between SES and delinquency. As Tittle and Meier (1990) point out, there is a need for researchers to investigate further the social class-crime link by devising unique strategies to uncover the causal process through which class affects crime. In the current study, one such strategy was used. Maternal work was measured both in terms of workplace controls and occupational complexity. These class-related measures, however, did not prove to influence delinquency.

On the other hand, a well-tested measure of social class, family income, did influence delinquency. This result is important because the connection between family income and delinquency contributes insight into the possible effects of maternal employment on youth crime. As argued by West (1982), maternal employment effectively increases family income, often preventing families from falling into abject poverty. In the current study, the family income variable included the earnings of both mothers and their spouses when present. In the case of a single mother, however, her income in many cases *is* the family income. As long as the earnings of women compare unfavorably to the income of men, single or divorced mothers often face a structural disadvantage when raising a family alone. If income does indeed influence delinquency, then efforts to improve the wages and occupational opportunities of women is an important policy issue.

Beyond the influence of family income on delinquency, a few significant effects of current maternal work were identified. First, as elsewhere in the analysis, welfare reliance was predictive of less warm and responsive parenting. In relation, increasing family income resulted in greater maternal warmth. This result is consistent with past work that has demonstrated that economic strains reduce parenting quality (McLoyd 1990).

Maternal supervision was influenced in an unexpected fashion by two current employment variables. First, in the current employment sample, the more hours mothers work, the greater the level of supervision they provide for their children. Although the positive effect of maternal hours worked on supervision is small in size, this finding is noteworthy because it contradicts past findings on this subject. Three major studies, in fact, reported that maternal employment actually increased delinquency by lowering maternal supervision (Glueck and Glueck 1950, Hirschi 1969, Sampson and Laub 1993).

The positive effect of hours on supervision found in this study, though very small, may be explained in the following way: the steadily employed parent must balance work and family responsibilities within the framework of a highly structured daily routine. A job "constitutes a framework for daily behavior and patterns of interaction because it imposes disciplines and regularities" upon the family (Wilson 1996, p. 73). Although satisfying the competing obligations of work and family may be an arduous task, employment may serve to make parenting a more disciplined, more efficient process. The organized and disciplined working mother may be more likely to effectively make a routine of the task of supervising her children.

In a contradictory finding, however, the present analysis identified bureaucratic workplace controls as having a negative effect on maternal supervision. One interpretation of this result is that professional mothers must invest more time in their careers than the average mother must. If professional mothers, for example, are more likely to function in a supervisory fashion at work and are more likely to travel as part of their job, then their ability to monitor and supervise their children may be diminished.

On the other hand, the negative relationship between bureaucratic work and supervision may not reflect a difference in time spent supervising children so much as it reflects parenting style. According to Kohn (1969), professional parents are more inclined to use normative control strategies with children as opposed to authoritarian controls. The freedom and autonomy enjoyed by a professional parent may translate into a parenting style characterized by the teaching and internalization of socially valued norms. The professional mother may practice less overt supervision because she believes that her children understand the value of conformity and are, therefore, more self-policing in their activities.

No other effects of current employment were detected in the analysis. In the next section, effects of delinquency pathways in adolescence are discussed.

Delinquency Risks in Adolescence

With respect to the adolescent delinquency pathways, several results of this analysis are consistent with past research that has identified certain variables as being important predictors of delinquent involvement. Consistent with dozens of studies on the causes of youth crime (e.g., Warr 1992), associations with delinquent peers was the strongest predictor of delinquency in this study. This finding supports the view that delinquent behaviors are learned in large part from one's peers and that friendships with delinquent others are important for the transmission and reinforcement of delinquent values and practices. More importantly for the purposes of this study, however, no link was identified between the employment status of one's mother and delinquent peer association. Notably, it was living in a socially disorganized neighborhood that seemed to make study children most vulnerable to delinquent peer association.

Also consistent with past research was the finding that attachment to school decreased delinquency. This finding supports a variety of theoretical positions, including Agnew's general strain theory (1992) and Hirschi's social bond perspective (1969). In Agnew's terms, school attachment might be seen as a type of positively valued stimuli that increases positive psychological affect and, thus, lowers the likelihood that individuals will react in an antisocial manner. Attachment to school might also be conceptualized as an important social bond. Those who like school and value their membership in school programs, clubs, and pro-social cliques are less likely to act in a delinquent manner because they have more to lose by getting caught and punished for their discretions. While this study did not identify the causal process through which school attachment decreases delinquency, it did show that mother's work had no impact on the extent to which children are satisfied with their school.

Finally, consistent with past research, higher maternal supervision proved to lower delinquent involvement. Parental supervision and monitoring has been characterized as a robust predictor of delinquency and the results of this analysis study support that view. It is important, then, that this study did not find maternal employment to have a weakening effect on supervision. Driven by the social control perspective, past researchers have often assumed that maternal employment is criminogenic because it lowers supervision (Glueck and Glueck 1950; Hirschi 1969). This study contradicts this belief.

As with any study, this analysis faced several limitations. First, while the NLSY sample is generally representative and contains variation in the work, family, and delinquency variables, it is not fully representative of the range of mothers and children in the United Stated for this time period. Most of the mothers investigated in this analysis were relatively early child bearers. As a result, women who postponed childbearing to pursue advanced education or to anchor themselves in careers were not included in the analysis. As Parcel and Menaghan (1994) note, many of these later child bearers are likely to be employed in jobs that are more complex, that are more stable, and that pay better. Including a larger range of later child bearers would increase the explanatory power of the analysis because it would raise the variation in both maternal employment and in maternal resources. Future work in this area should focus on a more diverse group of mothers as this may identify stronger effects of maternal employment (Parcel and Menaghan 1994).

Second, while the present study capitalized on the longitudinal nature of the NLSY to examine the importance of the timing of maternal employment, future efforts should be made to study the cumulative effects of maternal work over time. In this study, maternal employment was measured at two intervals, the pre-school years (4 to 6 year-olds) and early adolescence (12 to 14 year-olds). These age cohorts were selected because research and theory have suggested that these developmental periods are important for the transmission of parental control and support. The results of this analysis, however, do not lend themselves to interpretations of how maternal work affects family life and, ultimately, delinquency over a longer period of time. Coercive work, for example, might have a cumulative negative effect on family relations and adolescent behavior if mothers are constrained to working in such jobs over the length of their child's development. The same might be said of the possible cumulative negative effect of long-term welfare dependence or of the positive effects of long-term high quality employment. Future investigations into the impact of maternal work should be aimed at modeling the effects of mother's employment status throughout a child's early years and into adolescence.

Third, the issue of child care quality is inextricably linked with any questions about how maternal employment may affect child outcomes. Unfortunately, the NLSY data do not contain very detailed information on the types of daycare used by mothers. This study was constrained to using a series of dummy variables to control for very broad categorical variations in childcare. Richer data on the size, training, and resources of a daycare center or of the characteristics of an individual caregiver would shed light on the effects of nonparental care on child behavior.

Finally, future efforts should be made to study the relationship between maternal employment and delinquency on an older sample of children. In this study, the child sample is made up of twelve to fourteen year-olds, which presents problems in inferring my results to an older, more delinquency-prone age group (Farrington 1994). While this study is ostensibly about the factors that contribute to delinquency, delinquent involvement is generally low among the age group examined in this study. As a result, variation in the delinquency variable was relatively low. Furthermore, the delinquency index employed in this study was composed of relatively minor to moderate delinquent acts. While delinquency researchers commonly use these items, they are generally examined along with delinquent acts of greater severity.

The lack of serious delinquency in the dependent variable is significant because criminological theory often proposes that certain explanatory variables are more likely to be observed as predictors of serious or chronic delinquency. Colvin and Pauly (1983), for example, suggest that the children of fraction one workers (coercive work) are most likely to be involved in serious patterned delinquency, such as prolonged criminal violence, gang-related delinquency, or drug trade. Future work in this area should examine maternal work variables as they influence a broader variety of delinquent acts.

Policy Implications

While this study found few effects of maternal work on delinquency, there is evidence here that, for some groups, coercive work, welfare reliance, and lower family income are associated with lower quality parenting and negative child behavior. Taken together, these findings suggest that more children will be better off as women gain increased access to educational advancement, job training, and opportunities for stable, well-paying employment. As more women make the transition from welfare to work, it will be important to consider the quality and pay of the jobs that will replace welfare dependency for an entire generation of mothers and children. If workfare programs do provide job training, opportunities for advancement, and jobs with livable wages, then new welfare legislation will have helped to improve the lives of thousands of children. On the other hand, if yesterday's welfare recipients are more likely to find themselves today in dead-end secondary labor market jobs, then the next downturn in the economy might thrust many of them back into a life of poverty. The consequences of the recent welfare-to-work experiment may not be observable until shifts in the economy test the durability of workfare jobs.

Finally, this study contributes to the large body of research that suggests that maternal employment is not a risk factor for children. Policy debates focused on the reduction of youth crime, therefore, should avoid ideological attacks on mothers and concentrate instead on addressing other more important predictors of crime such as community breakdown, joblessness, and poverty. Stigmatizing the working mother will do little to change youth crime. On the contrary, a comprehensive program aimed at crime reduction would include broadening opportunities for women to find and maintain stable, high-paying jobs.

BIBLIOGRAPHY

Agnew, R. (1992) "Foundation for a General Strain Theory of Crime and Delinquency." *Criminology* 30:47-86.

Agnew, R. and H. R. White (1992) "An Empirical Test of General Strain Theory." *Criminology* 30:475-500.

Amato, P. R., Loomis, L. S., and A. Booth (1995) "Parental Divorce, Marital Conflict, and Offspring Well-being during Early Adulthood." *Social Forces* 73:895-915.

Aseltine, R. H. (1995) "A Reconsideration of Parental and Peer Influences on Adolescent Deviance." *Journal of Health and Social Behavior* 36:103-21.

Baker, R. L. and B. R. Mednick (1984) *Influences on Human Development: A Longitudinal Perspective.* Boston: Kluwer-Nijhoff.

Banducci, R. (1967) "The Effect of Mother's Employment on the Achievement, Aspirations, and Expectations of the Child." *Personnel and Guidance Journal* 46:263-67.

Barglow, P., Vaughn, B., and N. Molitor (1987) "Effects of Maternal Absence Due to Employment on the Quality of Infant-Mother Attachment in a Low-risk Sample." *Child Development* 58:945-54.

Barling, J. (1990) *Employment, Stress, and Family Functioning.* Chichester, England: John Wiley.

Barnett, R. C. and G. K. Baruch (1987) "Determinants of Father's Participation in Family Work." *Journal of Marriage and the Family* 49:29-40.

Baydar, N. and J. Brooks-Gunn (1991) "Effects of Maternal Employment and Child-care Arrangements on Preschoolers' Cognitive and Behavioral Outcomes: Evidence from the Children of the National Longitudinal Survey of Youth. *Developmental Psychology* 27:932-45.

Belknap, J. (1996) *The Invisible Woman: Gender, Crime and Justice.* Belmont, CA: Wadsworth Publishing Company.

Bellas, M. L. (1994) "Comparable Worth in Academia: The Effects on Faculty Salaries of the Sex Composition and Labor-Market Conditions of Academic Disciplines." *American Sociological Review* 59:807-821.

Belsky, J. (1988) "The 'Effects' of Infant Daycare Reconsidered." *Early Childhood Research Quarterly* 3:235-72.

Belsky, J. and J. M. Braungart (1991) "Are Insecure-Avoidant Infants with Extensive Day-Care Experience Less Stressed by and More Independent in the Strange Situation?" *Child Development* 62:567-71.

Belsky, J. and D. J. Eggebeen (1991) "Early and Extensive Maternal Employment and Young Children's Socioemotional Development: Children of the National Longitudinal Survey of Youth." *Journal of Marriage and the Family* 53:1083-1110.

Belsky. J. and M. Rovine (1988) "Nonmaternal Care in the First Year of Life and Infant-Parent Attachment Security." *Child Development* 59:157-76.

Benin, M. and V. M. Keith (1995) "The Social Support of Employed African American Mothers." *Journal of Family Issues* 16:275-297.

Benson, M. (2002) *Crime and the Life Course: An Introduction.* Los Angeles: Roxbury Publishing Company.

Blankenhorn, D. (1995) *Fatherless America: Confronting Our Most Urgent Social Problem.* New York: HarperCollins Publishers.

Blau, F. D. and M. A. Ferber (1986) *The Economics of Women, Men, and Work.* Englewood Cliffs, NJ: Prentice-Hall.

Brayfield, A. A., Deich, S. G., and S. L. Hofferth (1993) *Caring for Children in Low-Income Families: A Substudy of the National Child Care Survey, 1990.* Washington, D.C.: The Urban Institute Press.

Brody, G. and R. Forehand (1987) "Multiple Determinants of Parenting: The Divorce Process." In M. Hetherington and J. Arasteh (eds.), *Impact of Divorce, Single Parenting, and Stepparenting on Children.* Hillsdale: Erlbaum and Associates.

Broidy, L. M. (1995) "Direct Supervision and Delinquency: Assessing the Adequacy of Structural Proxies." *Journal of Criminal Justice* 23:541-554.

Bureau of Labor Statistics (2000) "Employment Characteristics of Families." In Bureau Of Labor Statistics News. Washington, D. C.: United States Department of Labor.

Canter, R. J. (1982) "Family Correlates of Male and Female Delinquency." *Criminology* 20:149-67.

Cernkovich, S. and P. Giordano (1987) "Family Relationships and Delinquency." *Criminology* 25:295-321.

Cernkovich, S., Giordano, P., and M. Pugh (1985) "Chronic Offenders: The Missing Cases in Self-Report Delinquency Research." *Journal of Criminal Law and Criminology* 76:705-32.

Chase-Lansdale, P. L. and M. T. Owen (1987) "Maternal Employment in a Family Context: Effects on Infant-Mother and Infant-Father Attachments. *Child Development* 58:1505-12.

Chase-Lansdale, P. L., Mott, F. L., Brooks-Gunn, J., and D. A. Phillips (1991) "Children of the National Longitudinal Survey of Youth: A Unique Research Opportunity." *Developmental Psychology* 27:918-31.

Cherlin, A. J. (1993) "Nostalgia as Family Policy." *Public Interest* 110:77-84.

Cherry, F. F. and E. L. Eaton (1977) "Physical and Cognitive Development in Children of Low-income Mothers Working in the Child's Early Years." *Child Development* 48:158-66.

Chira, S. (1998) *A Mother's Place.* NewYork: HarperCollins.

Chira, S. (1996) "Study Says Babies in Child Care Keep Secure Bonds to Mothers." *New York Times*, April 21, p. 1.

Cincinnati Post (1996) "The Latest From Marge: Women Belong at Home." May 14, section 1A.

Clarke-Stewart, K. A. (1988) "The 'Effects of Infant Daycare Reconsidered' Reconsidered: Risks for Parents, Children, and Researchers." *Early Childhood Research Quarterly* 3:293-318.

Clarke-Stewart, K. A. (1989) "Infant Day Care: Malignant or Maligned?" *American Psychologist* 44:266-73.

Cohen, R. A. (1996) "Women in the Service Occupation Sector." In P. Dubeck and K. Borman (eds.) *Women and Work: A Handbook.* New York: Garland.

Coleman, J. S. (1988) "Social Capital in the Creation of Human Capital." *American Journal of Sociology* 94:S95-S120.

Collins, R. and S. Coltrane (1995) *Sociology of Marriage and the Family,* fourth edition. Chicago: Nelson-Hall.

Colvin, M. (2000) *Crime and Coercion: An Integrated Theory of Chronic Criminality.* New York: St. Martin's.

Colvin, M. and J. Pauly (1983) "A Critique of Criminology: Toward an Integrated Structural-Marxist Theory of Delinquency Production." *American Journal of Sociology* 89:513-51.

Coverman, S. (1989) "Role Overload, Role Conflict, and Stress: Addressing Consequences of Multiple Role Demands." *Social Forces.* 67:965-82.

Crockenberg, S. (1988) "Stress and Role Satisfaction Experienced by Employed and Unemployed Mothers With Young Children." *Lifestyles: Family and Economic Issues* 9:97-110.

Crockenberg, S. and C. Litman (1991) "Effects of Maternal Employment on Maternal and Two-Year-Old Child Behavior." *Child Development* 62:930-53.

Cullen, F. T. (1994.) "Social Support as an Organizing Concept for Criminology: Presidential Address to the Academy of Criminal Justice Sciences." *Justice Quarterly* 11:527-59.

Cullen, F. T. and J. P. Wright (1997) "Liberating the Anomie-Strain Paradigm: Implications From Social Support Theory." In N. Passes and R. Agnew (eds.), *The Future of Anomie Theory.* Boston: Northeastern University Press.

Currie, E. (1985) *Confronting Crime: An American Challenge.* New York: Pantheon.

Currie, E. (1993) "Shifting the Balance: On Social Action and the Future of Criminological Research." *Journal of Research in Crime and Delinquency* 30:478-84.

Currie, E. (1998) *Crime and Punishment in America.* New York: Metropolitan Books.

Demo, D. H. (1992) "Parent-Child Relations: Assessing Recent Changes." *Journal of Marriage and the Family* 54:104-17.

Dionne, E.J. (2002) "The Motherhood Issue." *The Washington Post,* A33, July 26, 2002.

Dornbusch, S. M. (1989) "The Sociology of Adolescence." *Annual Review of Sociology* 15:233-59.

Dornbusch, S. M., Carlsmith, J. M., Bushwall, S. J., Ritter, P. L., Leiderman, H., Hastorf, A. H, and R. T. Gross (1985) "Single Parents, Extended Households, and the Control of Adolescents." *Child Development* 56:326-41.

Dubeck, P. J. and K. Borman, eds. (1996) *Women and Work: A Handbook.* New York: Garland.

Easterbrooks, M.A. and W.A. Goldberg (1985) "Effects of Early Maternal Employment on Toddlers, Mothers, and Fathers." *Developmental Psychology* 21:774-83.

Easterbrooks, M. A. and W. A. Goldberg (1988) "Security of Toddler-Parent Attachment: Relation to Children's Sociopersonality Functioning During Kindergarten." In M. Greenberg, D. Cicchetti, and M. Cummings (eds.), *Attachment in the Preschool Years: Theory, Research and Intervention.* Chicago: University of Chicago Press. Pages

Eckenrode, J and S. Gore (1990) "Stress and Coping at the Boundary of Work and Family" In J. Eckenrode and S. Gore (eds.), *Stress Between Work and Family*, pp. 39-60. New York: Plenum Press.

Edin, K. and L. Lein (1997) *Making Ends Meet.* New York: Russell Sage Foundation.

Edwards, R. (1979) *Contested Terrain.* New York: Basic Books.

Elliott, D. S. and D. Huizinga (1989) "Improving Self-Reported Measures of Delinquency." In M. W. Klein (ed.), *Cross-National Research in Self-Reported Crime and Delinquency.* Dordrecht, Netherlands: Kluwer.

Elliott, D. S. and H. L. Voss (1974) *Delinquency and Dropout.* Lexington, MA: D.C. Heath.

Elliott, D. S., D. Huizinga and S. S. Ageton (1985) *Explaining Delinquency and Drug Use.* Beverly Hills: Sage.

England, P. (1994) "Foreword." Pp. xii-xiii in T. L. Parcel and E. G. Menaghan, *Parents' Jobs and Children's Lives.* New York: Aldine De Gruyter.

England, P., M. S. Herbert, B. S. Kilbourne, L. L. Reid, and L. M. Megdal (1994) "The Gendered Valuation of Occupations and Skills: Earnings in 1980 Census Occupations." *Social Forces* 73:65-99.

Erikson, E. H. ([1959] 1994) *Identity and the Life Cycle.* New York: W. Norton and Company.

Fahey, T. W. (1995) *The National Longitudinal Surveys of Labor Market Experience: An Annotated Bibliography of Research.* Bureau of Labor Statistics, U.S. Department of Labor.

Farnworth, M. (1984) "Family Structure, Family Attributes, and Delinquency in a Sample of Low-Income, Minority Males and Females." *Journal of Youth and Adolescence* 13:349-64.

Farrell, M. P., G. M. Barnes, and S. Banerjee (1995) "Family Cohesion as a Buffer Against the Effects of Problem-Drinking Fathers on Psychological Distress, Deviant Behavior, and Heavy Drinking Adolescents." *Journal of Health and Social Behavior* 36:377-85.

Farrington, D. P. (1986) "Stepping Stones to Adult Criminal Careers."
    In D. Olweus, J. Block, and M.R. Yarrow (eds.), *Development of
    Antisocial and Prosocial Behavior*. New York: Academic Press.
    PAGES
    _____ (1994) "Human Development and Criminal Careers." In
    M. Maguire, R. Morgan, and R. Rainer (eds.), *The Oxford
    Handbook of Criminology*, pp. 511-84. New York: Oxford
    University Press.
Farrington, D. P., R. Loeber, M. Stouthamer-Loeber, W. B. Van
    Kammen, and L. Scmidt (1996) "Self-Reported Delinquency and a
    Combined Delinquency Seriousness Scale Based on Boys,
    Mothers, and Teachers: Concurrent and Predictive Validity for
    African-Americans and Caucasians." *Criminology* 34:493-514.
Fierman, J. (1990) "Why Women Still Don't Hit the Top." *Fortune*.
    July 30.
Fisher, S. (1985) "Control and Blue Collar Work." In C. L. Cooper and
    M. J. Smith (eds.), *Job Stress and Blue Collar Work*. Wiley: New
    York.
Fox, N. and G. Fein (eds.) (1990) *Infant Day Care: The Current
    Debate*. Norwood, NJ: Ablex.
Furstenberg, F. F., Jr. (1994) "Good Dads-Bad Dads: Two Faces of
    Fatherhood." In A. S. Skolnick and J.H. Skolnick (eds.), *Family in
    Transition*, eighth edition. New York: HarperCollins. PAGES
Furstenberg, F. F., Jr. and A. J. Cherlin (1991) *Divided Families: What
    Happens to Children When Parents Part*. Cambridge, MA:
    Harvard University Press.
Gamble, T. J. and E. Zigler (1986) "Effects of Infant Day Care:
    Another Look at the Evidence." *American Journal of
    Orthopsychiatry* 56:26-42.
Gamst, F.C. (1995) *Meanings of Work: Considerations for the Twenty-
    First Century*. Albany, NY: State University of New York Press.
Gelles, R. J. (1978) "Violence Towards Children in the United States."
    Journal of Orthopsychiatry 48:580-92.
Gerson, K. (1996) "Gender and the Future of the Family: Implications
    For the Post-Industrial Workplace." Conference paper presented
    at the Agenda for the 21st Century Labor Force Meeting,
    Cincinnati, OH. November 15-17, 1996.

Giles-Sims, J., M. A. Straus, and D. B. Sugarman (1995) "Child, Maternal, and Family Characteristics Associated with Spanking." *Family Relations* 44:170-6.

Gill, R. T. (1993) "Family Breakdown as Family Policy." *Public Interest* 110:84-91.

Glueck, S. and E. Glueck. (1950) *Unraveling Juvenile Delinquency.* Cambridge, MA: Harvard University Press.

Goldberg, W. A. and M. A. Easterbrooks (1988) "Maternal Employment When Children Are Toddlers and Kindergarteners." In A. E. Gottfried and A. W. Gottfried (eds.), *Maternal Employment and Children's Development: Longitudinal Research*, pp. 121-154. New York: Plenum.

Goldberger L. and S. Breznitz (1982) *Handbook of Stress: Theoretical and Clinical Aspects.* New York: Free Press.

Gormley, W. T. (1995) *Everybody's Children: Child Care as a Public Problem.* Washington, DC: Brookings Institution.

Gottfredson, M. and T. Hirschi (1990) *A General Theory of Crime.* Stanford: Stanford University Press.

Gottfried, A. E., Gottfried, A. W., and K. Bathurst (1988) "Maternal Employment, Family Environment and Children's Development: Infancy Through the School Years." In A. E. Gottfried and A. W. Gottfried (eds.), *Maternal Employment and Children's Development: Longitudinal Research*, pp. 11-58. New York: Plenum.

Gove, W. and R. D. Crutchfield (1982) "The Family and Juvenile Delinquency." *The Sociological Quarterly* 23:301-19.

Greenberger, E. and W. A. Goldberg (1989) "Work, Parenting, and the Socialization of Children." *Developmental Psychology* 25:22-35.

Greenberger, E., Goldberg, W. A., Crawford, T., and J. Granger (1988) "Beliefs About the Consequences of Maternal Employment for Children." *Psychology of Women Quarterly.* 12:35-59.

Greenstein, T. N. (1993) "Maternal Employment and Child Behavioral Outcomes: A Household Economics Analysis." *Journal of Family Issues* 14: 323-54.

Greenstein, T. N. (1995) "Are the 'Most Advantaged' Children Truly Disadvantaged by Early Maternal Employment?" *Journal of Family Issues* 16:149-69.

Hagan, J., Gillis, A., and J. Simpson (1985) "The Class Structure of Gender and Delinquency: Toward a Power-Control Theory of

Gender and Delinquency." *American Journal of Sociology* 90:1151-78.

Hagan, J., Gillis, A., and J. Simpson (1987) "Class in the Household: A Power-Control Theory of Gender and Delinquency." *American Journal of Sociology* 92:788-817.

Hagan, J., Gillis, A., and J. Simpson (1990) "Clarifying and Extending Power-Control Theory." *American Journal of Sociology* 95:1024-37.

Hall, C. (1995) "Women's Income Essential." *USA Today*, December 22, section A, p. 1.

Hanson, S. L. and D. M. Sloane (1992) "Young Children and Job Satisfaction." *Journal of Marriage and the Family* 54:799-811.

Harvey, E. (1999) "Long-Term Effects of Early Parental Employment on Children of the NLSY." *Developmental Psychology*, 35:445-59.

Haskins, R. (1985) "Public School Aggression Among Children With Varying Day-Care Experience." *Child Development* 56: 689-703.

Haurin, R. J. (1992) "Patterns of Childhood Residence and the Relationship to Young Adult Outcomes." *Journal of Marriage and the Family* 54:846-60.

Hetherington, E. M., (1981) In R. Henderson (ed.), *Parent-Child Interaction: Theory, Research and Prospects.* New York: Academic Press.

Heyns, B. (1982) "The Influence of Parents' Work on Children's School Achievement." In S. B. Kamerman and C. D. Hayes (eds.), *Families That Work: Children in a Changing World*, pp. 229-67. Washington, D.C.: National Academy Press.

Heyns, B. and S. Catsambis (1986) "Working Mothers and the Achievement of Children: A Critique." *Sociology of Education* 59:140-51.

Hillman, S. B. and S. S. Sawilowsky. (1991) "Maternal Employment and Early Adolescent Substance Use." *Adolescence* 26:829-37.

Hindelang, M. J. (1971) "Age, Sex, and the Versatility of Delinquent Involvements." *Social Problems* 18:522-35.

Hindelang, M. J., Hirschi, T. and J. G. Weis (1981) *Measuring Delinquency*. Beverly Hills, CA: Sage.

Hirschi, T. (1969) *Causes of Delinquency.* Berkeley: University of California Press.

Hodson, R. (1989) "Gender Differences in Job Satisfaction: Why Aren't Women More Dissatisfied?" *Sociological Quarterly* 30:385-99.

Hodson, R. and T. A. Sullivan (1990) *The Social Organization of Work*. Belmont, CA: Wadsworth.

Hoffman, L. W. (1983) "Increasing Fathering: Effects on the Mother." In M. Lamb and A. Sagi (eds.), *Fatherhood and Family Policy*, pp. 167-90. Hillsdale, NJ: Lawrence Erlbaum Associates.

Hoffman, L. W. (1984) "Work, Family, and the Socialization of the Child." In R. Parke (ed.), *Review of Child Development Research*, pp. 223-82. Chicago: University of Chicago Press.

Hoffman, L. W. (1986) "Work, Family, and the Child." In M.S. Pallak and R.O. Perloff (eds.), *Psychology and Work: Productivity, Change and Employment*, pp. 173-220. Washington, DC: American Psychological Association.

Hoffman, L. W. (1989) "Effects of Maternal Employment in the Two-Parent Family." *American Psychologist* 44:283-92.

Howes, C. and M. Olenick (1986) "Family and Child Care Influences on Toddler's Compliance." *Child Development* 57:202-16.

Jacobs, J. A. and R. J. Steinberg (1990) "Compensating Differentials and the Male-Female Wage-Gap: Evidence from the New York State Comparable Worth Study." *Social Forces* 69:439-68.

Jacobson, J. L. and D. E. Wille (1984) "Influence of Attachment and Separation Experience on Separation Distress at 18 Months." *Developmental Psychology* 20:477-84.

Jenchura, J. (1995) "In Defense of Working Moms." *Wall Street Journal*, November 14, section A, p. 15.

Johnson, R. E. (1986) "Family Structure and Delinquency: General Patterns and Gender Differences." *Criminology* 24:64-84.

Johnson, R. E, Marcos, A. C., and S. J. Bahr (1987) "The Role of Peers in the Complex Etiology of Adolescent Drug Use." *Criminology* 25:323-39.

Kercher, K. (1988) "Criminology." In E. F. Borgatta and K. S. Cook (eds.), *The Future of Sociology*, pp. 294-316. Beverly Hills, CA: Sage.

Kessler, R., Turner, J. B. and J. S. House. (1988) Effects of Unemployment on Health in a Community Survey: Main, Modifying, and Mediating Effects." *Journal of Social Issues* 44:69-85.

King, V. (1994) "Variation in the Consequences of Nonresident Father Involvement for Children's Well-Being." *Journal of Marriage and the Family* 56:963-72.

Kobak, R. R. and A. Sceery (1988) "Attachment in Late Adolescence: Working Models, Affect Regulation, and Representations of Self and Others." *Child Development* 59:135-46.

Kohn, M. L. (1977) *Class and Conformity, A Study in Values,* Second Edition. Chicago: University of Chicago Press.

Kohn M. L. and C. Schooler (1982) "Job Conditions and Personality: A Longitudinal Assessment of Their Reciprocal Effects." *American Journal of Sociology* 87:1257-86.

Kolvin, I., Miller, F. J. W., Fleeting, M., and P. A. Kolvin (1988) "Risk/protective Factors for Offending With Particular Reference to Deprivation" In M. Rutter (ed.), *Studies of Psychosocial Risk: The Power of Longitudinal Data,* pp. 77-95. New York: Cambridge University Press.

Kristol, I. (1996) "Sex Trumps Gender." *Wall Street Journal,* March 6, section A, p. 20.

Lamb, M. E., ed. (1981) *The Role of the Father in Child Development,* 2nd Edition. New York: Wiley.

Larner, M. and D. Phillips (1994) "Defining and Valuing Quality as a Parent." In P. Moss and A. Pence (eds.), *Valuing Quality in Early Childhood Services,* pp. 43-60. New York: Teachers College Press.

Lennon, M. C. (1994) "Women, Work, and Well-Being: The Importance of Work Conditions." *Journal of Health and Social Behavior* 35:235-47.

Link, B. G., Lennon, M. C. and B. P. Dohrenwend (1993) "Socioeconomic Status and Depression: The Role of Occupations Involving Direction, Control, and Planning." *American Journal of Sociology* 98:1351-87.

Loeber, R. and T. Dishion (1983) "Early Predictors of Male Delinquency: A Review." *Psychological Bulletin* 94:68-99.

Loeber, R. and M. Le Blanc (1990) "Toward a Developmental Criminology." In M. Tonry and N. Morris (eds.), *Crime and Justice: A Review of Research,* vol. 12, pp. 375-473. Chicago: University of Chicago Press.

Loeber, R. and M. Stouthamer-Loeber (1986) "Family Factors as Correlates and Predictors of Juvenile Conduct Problems and

Delinquency." In M. Tonry and N. Morris (eds.), *Crime and Justice: An Annual Review of Research, Vol. 7.* Chicago: University of Chicago Press.

Louv, R (1990) *Childhood's Future.* New York: Anchor Books.

Luster, T. and H. P. McAdoo (1994) "Factors Related to the Achievement and Adjustment of Young African American Children." *Child Development* 65:1080-94.

MacEwen, K. E. and J. Barling (1991) "Effects of Maternal Employment Experiences on Children's Behavior via Mood, Cognitive Difficulties, and Parenting Behavior." *Journal of Marriage and the Family* 53:635-44.

McLanahan, S. and K. Booth (1989) "Mother-Only Families: Problems, Prospects, and Politics.' *Journal of Marriage and the Family* 51:557-80.

McLeod, J. D., Kruttschnitt, C. and M. Dornfeld (1994) "Does Parenting Explain the Effects of Structural Conditions on Children's Antisocial Behavior? A Comparison of Blacks and Whites." *Social Forces* 73(2): 575-604.

McLoyd, V. C. (1989) "Socialization and Development in a Changing Economy." *American Psychologist* 44:293-302.

_____ (1990) "The Impact of Economic Hardship on Black Families and Children: Psychological Distress, Parenting, and Socioemotional Development." *Child Development* 61:311-46.

Mednick, M. T. (1994) "Single Mothers: A Review and Critique of Current Research." In A.S. Skolnick and J.H. Skolnick (eds.), *Family in Transition*, eighth edition. New York: HarperCollins.

Menaghan, E. G. (1991) "Work Experiences and Family Interaction Processes: The Long Reach of the Job? *Annual Review of Sociology* 17:19-44.

Menaghan, E. G. and T. L. Parcel (1991) "Determining Children's Home Environments: The Impact of Maternal Characteristics and Current Occupational and Family Conditions." *Journal of Marriage and the Family* 53:417-31.

Menaghan, E. G., Kowaleski-Jones, L., and F. L. Mott (1997) "The Intergenerational Costs of Parental Social Stressors: Academic and Social Difficulties in Early Adolescence for Children of Young Mothers." *Journal of Health and Social Behavior* 38:72-86.

Messner, S. F. and M. D. Krohn (1990) "Class, Compliance Structures, and Delinquency: Assessing Integrated Structural-Marxist Theory." *American Journal of Sociology* 96:300-28.

Milne, A. M., Myers, D. E., Rosenthal, A. S., and A. Ginsburg (1986) "Single Parents, Working Mothers, and the Educational Achievement of School Children" *Sociology of Education* 59:125-39.

Mohan, P. J. (1990) "The Effect of Maternal Employment on Mormon and Non-Mormon Adolescents." *Adolescence* 100:832-37.

Montemayor, R. (1984) "Maternal Employment and Adolescents' Relations With Parents, Siblings, and Peers." *Journal of Youth and Adolescence* 13:543-57.

Moorehouse, M. J. (1991) "Linking Maternal Employment Patterns to Mother-Child Activities and Children's School Competence." *Developmental Psychology* 27:295-303.

Morash, M. and L. Rucker (1989) "An Exploratory Study of the Connection of Mother's Age at Childbearing to Her Children's Delinquency in Four Data Sets." *Crime and Delinquency* 35:45-93.

Mortimer, J. T. and J. Lorence (1995) "Social Psychology of Work." In K.S. Cook, G.A. Fine, J.S. House (eds.), *Sociological Perspectives on Social Psychology*, pp. 497-523. Boston: Allyn and Bacon.

Moss, P. and A. Pence, eds. (1994) *Valuing Quality in Early Childhood Services.* New York: Teachers College Press.

Mott, F. L. (1991) "Developmental Effects of Infant Care: Mediating Role of Gender and Health." *Journal of Social Issues* 47:139-58.

Mott, F. L. (1995) *The NLSY Children 1992: Description and Evaluation.* Columbus, OH: Center for Human Resource Research.

Muller, C. (1995) "Maternal Employment, Paternal Involvement, and Mathematics Achievement Among Adolescents." *Journal of Marriage and the Family* 57:85-100.

Nock, S. L. and P. W. Kingston (1984) "The Family Work Day." *Journal of Marriage and the Family* 46:333-43.

Nye, F. I. (1963) In F.I. Nye and L. Hoffman (eds.), *The Employed Mother in America*, pp. 165-81. Chicago: Rand McNally.

Owen, M. T. and M. J. Cox (1988) "Maternal Employment and the Transition to Parenthood." In A. E. Gottfried and A. W. Gottfried (eds.), *Maternal Employment and Children's Development: Longitudinal Research*, pp. 85-119. New York: Plenum.

Owen, M. T., Easterbrooks, M. A., Chase-Lansdale, L., and W. A. Goldberg (1984) "The Relation Between Maternal Employment Status and the Stability of Attachment to Mother and to Father." *Child Development* 55: 1894-1901.

Parcel, T. L. (1996) "Working Mothers, Welfare Mothers: Implications For Children in the 21st Century." Conference paper presented at the Agenda for the 21st Century Labor Force Meeting, Cincinnati, OH. November 15-17, 1996.

Parcel, T. L. and E. G. Menaghan (1990) "Maternal Working Conditions and Children's Verbal Facility: Studying the Intergenerational Transmission of Inequality from Mothers to Young Children." *Social Psychology Quarterly* 53:132-47.

Parcel, T. L. and E. G. Menaghan (1994) *Parents' Jobs and Children's Lives*. New York: Aldine De Gruyter.

Parcel, T. L. and E. G. Menaghan (1994) "Early Parental Work, Family Social Capital, and Early Childhood Outcomes." *American Journal of Sociology* 99:972-1009.

Parcel, T. L., R. A. Nickoll, and M. J. Dufur (1996) "The Effects of Parental Work and Maternal Nonemployment on Children's Reading and Math Achievement." *Work and Occupations* 23:461-83.

Patterson, G. R. (1982) *A Social Learning Approach: Coercive Family Process, Vol. 3*. Eugene, OR: Castalia.

Paulson, S. E. (1996) "Maternal Employment and Adolescent Achievement Revisited: An Ecological Perspective." *Family Relations* 45:201-08.

Pearlin, L. I. and M. M. McCall. 1990. "Occupational Stress and Marital Support: A Description of Microprocesses." In J. Eckenrode and S. Gore (eds.), *Stress Between Work and Family*, pp. 39-60. New York: Plenum Press.

Pett, M. A.., B. Vaughan-Cole, and B. E. Wampold (1994) "Maternal Employment and Perceived Stress: Their Impact on Children's Adjustment and Mother-Child Interaction in Young Divorced and Married Families." *Family Relations* 43:151-58.

Pleck, J. H. (1983) "Husbands' Paid Work and Family Roles: Current Research Issues." In H.Z. Lopata and J.H. Pleck (eds.), *Research in the Interweave of Social Roles,* pp. 251-333. Greenwich CT: JAI Press.

Poponoe, D. (1993) "American Family Decline, 1960-1990: A Review and Appraisal." *Journal of Marriage and the Family* 55:527-55.

Reeves, D. L. (1992) *Child Care Crisis.* Santa Barbara: ABC-CLIO, Inc.

Reige, M. (1972) "Parental Affection and Juvenile Delinquency in Girls." *British Journal of Criminology* 12:55-73.

Reskin, B. and I. Padavic (1994) *Women and Men at Work.* Thousand Oaks, CA: Pine Forge Press.

Richards, M. H. and E. Duckett (1994.) "The Relationship of Maternal Employment to Early Adolescent Daily Experience With and Without Parents." *Child Development* 65:225-36.

Rogers, S. J. (1996) "Mothers' Work Hours and Marital Quality: Variations by Family Structure and Family Size." *Journal of Marriage and the Family* 58:606-17.

Rogers, S. J., Parcel, T. L. and E. G. Menaghan (1991) "The Effects of Maternal Working Conditions and Mastery on Child Behavior Problems: Studying the Intergenerational Transmission of Social Control." *Journal of Health and Social Behavior* 32 (June):145-64.

Rosen, L. (1985) "Family and Delinquency: Structure or Function?" *Criminology* 23:553-73.

Rosenfeld, R. (1980) "Race and Sex Differences in Career Dynamics." *American Sociological Review* 45: 583-609.

Rossi, A. (1985) "Gender and Parenthood." In A. Rossi (ed.), *Gender and the Life Course*, pp. 161-91. Hawthorne, NY: Aldine.

Roy, P. (1963) "Adolescent Roles: Rural-urban Differentials." In F.I. Nye and L. Hoffman (eds.), *The Employed Mother in America*, pp. 165-81. Chicago: Rand McNally.

Sampson, R. J. and J. H. Laub (1993) *Crime in the Making: Pathways and Turning Points Through Life.* Cambridge, MA: Harvard University Press.

Sampson, R. J. and J. H. Laub (1994) "Urban Poverty and the Family Context of Delinquency: A New Look at Structure and Process in a Classic Study." *Child Development* 65:523-40.

Scarr, S and M. Eisenberg (1993) "Child Care Research: Issues, Perspectives, and Results." *Annual Review of Psychology* 44:613-44.

Scarr, S., Phillips, D., and K. McCartney (1994) "Working Mothers and Their Families." In A.S. Skolnick and J.H. Skolnick (eds.), *Family in Transition*, eighth edition. New York: HarperCollins.

Schroeder, L. D., Sjoquist, D. L., and P. E. Stephan (1986) *Understanding Regression Analysis.* Newbury Park, CA: Sage.

Schwarz, J. C., Strickland, R. C., and G. Krolick (1974) "Infant Day Care: Behavioral Effects at Pre-school Age." *Developmental Psychology* 10: 502-06.

Schwartz, P. (1983) "Length of Day Care Attendance and Attachment Behavior in 18-month-old Infants." *Child Development* 54: 1073-78.

Seyler, D. L., Monroe, P. A., and J. C. Garand (1995) "Balancing Work and Family: The Role of Employer-Supported Child Care Benefits." *Journal of Family Issues* 16: 170-193.

Sherman, A., Amey, C., Duffield, B., Ebb, N., and D. Weinstein. (1998) *Welfare to What?: Early Findings on Family Hardship and Well-being.* Washington, D.C.: Children's Defense Fund and National Coalition for the Homeless.

Siegal, M. (1984) "Economic Deprivation and the Quality of Parent-Child Relations: A Trickle-Down Framework." *Journal of Applied Developmental Psychology* 5:127-44.

Simons, R. L., Whitbeck, L. B., Beaman, J., and R. D. Conger (1994) "The Impact of Mothers' Parenting, Involvement by Nonresidential Fathers, and Parental Conflict on the Adjustment of Adolescent Children." *Journal of Marriage and the Family* 94:356-74.

Simpson, S. S. and L. Elis (1994) "Is Gender Subordinate to Class? An Empirical Assessment of Colvin and Pauly's Structural Marxist Theory of Delinquency." *The Journal of Criminal Law and Criminology* 85:453-70.

Silverstein, L. B. (1991) "Transforming the Debate About Child Care and Maternal Employment." *American Psychologist* 46:1025-32.

Stacey, J. (1993) "Good Riddance to 'The Family': A Response to Poponoe." *Journal of Marriage and the Family* 55: 545-47.

Steinmetz, S. K. (1979) "Disciplinary Techniques and Their Relationship to Aggressiveness, Dependency, and Conscience." In

W. R. Burr, R. Hill, F. I. Nye, and I. I. Reiss (eds.), *Contemporary Theories about the Family*, pp. 165-81. New York: Free Press.

Stifter, C. A., Coulehan, C. M. and M. Fish (1993) "Linking Employment to Attachment: The Mediating Effects of Maternal Separation Anxiety and Interactive Behavior." *Child Development* 64:145-60.

Stipek, D. and J. McCroskey (1989) "Investing in Children: Government and Workplace Policies for Parents." *American Psychologist* 44:416-23.

Straus, M. A. (1991) "Discipline and Deviance: Physical Punishment of Children and Violence and Other Crime in Adulthood." *Social Problems* 38:133-54.

Strong, M. M. (1995) "In Defense of Working Moms." *Wall Street Journal*, November 14, section A, p. 14.

Strubel, A. (1996) "What's a Woman To Do, Mr. Kristol?" *Wall Street Journal*, March 18, section A, p. 19.

Suffolk Life. 1999. "Working Moms." 8M, June 30.

Symonds, A. (1995) "'Me Generation' Parents Should Grow Up." *Wall Street Journal*, October 31, section A.

Sutherland, E. (1939) *Principles of Criminology*. Philadelphia: Lippincott.

Sykes, G. M. and F. T. Cullen (1992) *Criminology*. Fort Worth, TX: Harcourt Brace Jovanovich College Publishers.

Thomas, G., Farrell, M. P., and G. M. Barnes (1996) "The Effects of Single-Mother Families and Nonresident Fathers on Delinquency and Substance Abuse in Black and White Adolescents." *Journal of Marriage and the Family* 58:884-94.

Thornberry, T. P., Moore, M., and R. L. Christenson (1985) "The Effect of Dropping Out of High School on Subsequent Criminal Behavior." *Criminology* 23:3-18.

Tschann, J. M., Johnston, J. R., Kline, M., and J. S. Wallerstein (1989) "Family Process and Children's Functioning During Divorce." *Journal of Marriage and the Family* 51:431-44.

Turner, R. J., Wheaton, B. and D. A. Lloyd (1995) "The Epidemiology of Social Stress." *American Sociological Review* 60:104-25.

U.S. Bureau of Census (1993) *Statistical Abstract of the United States*, 113th ed. Washington, D.C.: U.S. Government Printing Office.

Users Guide (1997) *1994 Child and Young Adult Data*. Bureau of Labor Statistics, U.S. Department of Labor.

Vandell, D. L. and J. Ramanan (1992) "Effects of Early and Recent Maternal Employment on Children from Low-Income Families." *Child Development* 63:938-49.

Vannoy, D. and W. M. Philliber (1992) "Wife's Employment and Quality of Marriage." *Journal of Marriage and the Family* 54:387-98.

Van Voorhis, P., Cullen, F. T., Mathers, R. A., and C. C. Garner (1988) "The Impact of Family Structure and Quality on Delinquency: A Comparative Assessment of Structure and Functional Factors." *Criminology* 26:235-61.

Vaughn, B., Gore, F., and B. Egeland (1980) "The Relationship Between Out-of-home-care and the Quality of Infant-Mother Attachment in an Economically Disadvantaged Population." *Child Development* 51:1203-14.

Voydanoff, P. (1987) *Work and Family Life*. Beverly Hills, CA: Sage.

Warr, M. (1993) "Age, Peers, and Delinquency." *Criminology* 31:17-40.

Warr, M. (1993) "Parents, Peers, and Delinquency." *Social Forces* 72:247-64.

Warren, J.A. and P.J. Johnson (1993) "The Impact of Workplace Support on Work-Family Strain." *Family Relations* 44:163-69.

Weinraub, M. and B. M. Wolf (1983) Effects of Stress Social Supports on Mother-Child Interaction in Single and Two-Parent Families." *Child Development* 54:1297-1311.

Wells, L. E. and J. H. Rankin (1988) "Direct Parental Controls and Delinquency." *Criminology* 26(2):263-85.

Wells, L. E. and J. H. Rankin (1991) "Families and Delinquency: A Meta-Analysis of the Impact of Broken Homes." *Social Problems* 38:71-93.

West, D. J. (1982) *Delinquency: Its Roots, Careers and Prospects*. Cambridge, MA: Harvard University Press.

West, D. J. and D. P. Farrington (1977) *The Delinquent Way of Life*. London: Heinemann.

Wiatrowski, M. D., Griswold, D. B., and M. K. Roberts (1981) "Social Control Theory and Delinquency." *American Sociological Review* 46:525-41.

Wilson, J. Q. (1993) "The Family-Values Debate." *Commentary* 95:24-31.

Wilson, J. Q. and R. J. Herrnstein (1985) *Crime and Human Nature.* New York: Simon and Schuster.

Wright, J. P. (1996) "Parental Support and Juvenile Delinquency: A Test of Social Support Theory." Unpublished Ph. D. study, University of Cincinnati.

Zaslow, M. J., Pederson, F. A., Suwalsky, J. T .D., Cain, R. L., and M. Fivel (1985) "The Early Resumption of Employment by Mothers: Implications for Parent-Child Interaction." *Journal of Applied Developmental Psychology* 6:1-16.

Zhao, J., J. Cao, and L. Cao (1997) "The Effects of Female Headship and Welfare on Delinquency: An Analysis of Five-Wave Panel Data." Presented at the Academy of Criminal Justice Sciences Meeting, Louisville, KY, Spring 1997.

Zigler E. F. (1994) "Addressing the Nation's Child Care Crisis: The School of the Twenty-first Century." In J.H. Skolnick and E. Currie (eds.), *Crisis in American Institutions*, pp. 255-64. New York: Harper Collins.

INDEX